RADIANCE OF BEING

RADIANCE OF BEING

pointers to self-knowing

by Rodney Stevens

Epigraph Books
Rhinebeck, New York

Paperback ISBN: 978-1-944037-52-9
eBook ISBN: 978-1-944037-53-6

Library of Congress Control Number: 2016959939

Epigraph Books
22 East Market Street, Suite 304
Rhinebeck, NY 12572
USA
(845) 876-4861
www.epigraphps.com

All text is from Rodney's blog on non-duality, 'Radiance of Being',
http://radianceofbeing.blogspot.nl/.
Most bold / italicized text as well as slightest editing by
André van den Brink.

"Realization is the discovery of the timeless factor in every experience.
It is awareness which makes the experience possible."

NISARGADATTA MAHARAJ

Don't attempt to repeat
or memorize these pointers.
Rather, let them resonate within you.
You may even try putting them aside for a while
and then re-reading them.
Coming upon them afresh may allow you to see, directly
and unequivocally, the awareness to
which they are pointing.

◆ Pointers have two functions: To point to truth, and to negate what **appears** to be truth.

◆ These pointers are directing you to your existing nature and not to some mystical or faraway state. You are awareness **right now**! At various times during the day, you may have a strong sense or inkling of this fact. Remain with that inkling and let it direct you to your own immeasurableness.

◆ See or feel what the pointer is pointing to. The words are nudging you (directionally, not sequentially) towards a peace and silence that has been glaringly overlooked. You **are** that silence! You **are** that peace! And even those descriptions are concepts on top of the indescribable **This**-ness of presence.

◆ All pointers here are pointing to something that is immediate, actual, and without beginning or end. I have zero interest in theories and conjecture. For, **before** any concept or idea can pop up into your head, you are awareness **already**. Just confirm it for yourself.

◆ The world is not the problem, and neither are you. This understanding is simply about your recognizing the fact that what you are seeking is precisely what you are right now!

3

◆   The first step to enlightenment is to see that there are no steps whatsoever, and that there is no one to get enlightened.

◆   There are no grades or levels to our natural state. No person is more 'enlightened' than the other. Buddha's and Christ's understanding is the same as Nisargadatta's and Bob Adamson's. However, each person *expresses* that understanding differently. And there certainly may be varying experiences *before* self-realization. But these events do not *lead* to your cognitizing presence. That can only be done immediately, *tout de suite*. But most seekers not only long for experiences, they want the exact ones that they have heard and read about from popular spiritual writers and teachers. But such endeavours are unavailing. For experiences, however spectacular, are temporary. Thus, they can never be the essence of what you *are*.

◆   *Kundalini* surges and seeing auras are on the same level as blissful meditative states: They are all experiences. They have no causal relationship to awareness—your true identity. So basically, they are just a waste of time. If they occur, so be it. Merely see them for what they are: passing appearances—and continue with your investigation into the actuality of your natural state.

◆ Experiences, though, can be instrumental in spurring one on to true self-knowledge. I know that that was certainly the case with me. But no experience, however psychic or visionary, was captivating enough to pull me away from this quest for a fundamental understanding of both myself and of life. And I was certainly guilty—all of those years ago—of labelling the intention of that quest as 'enlightenment'. But in the spring of 2007, I clearly saw that there is no separate individual to be enlightened at all! All there was was my natural state, which was one of enduring peace and spaciousness. And that natural state was pristine awareness, from which one never moves. So you are *already* what you are seeking. Thus, any notions of practices, methods, or spiritual journeys can simply be thrown out of the window.

◆ With self-knowing, you don't reach the end of a path— the path disappears. You simply see that it was never there in the first place. It was your own creation.

◆ Non-duality is a timeless teaching that points to the fact that the totality of existence is nothing but awareness.

◆ Self-realization is, quite literally, non-duality.

◆ The fundamental question in philosophy is, 'What is truth?' And non-duality is the answer to that question. For it is truth itself.

◆ Don't read non-dual books just for knowledge. See what the words are pointing to. And what they are pointing to is any pause, stillness, or penetrating insight. Bring your full attention to any of these, and freedom can be found.

◆ You can talk about advaitic / non-dual theory all day long—anyone can do that. But how are you helped by it? You are simply left with more questions. The only thing that leaves you without a single doubt is the recognition of your natural state.

◆ *Rodney*: Non-dual sages and scripture tell us that there are **no two things** in the universe. See the awe and beauty of this: There are no two things in the entire universe! *All is awareness*. So what is it, right now, that is fully present, but is not an object?

Q: *Presence itself.*

Rodney: And presence is totally without attributes or qualities. Yet, it manifests itself through our ephemeral bodies and minds as unwavering equanimity and spaciousness.

◆ See right at this moment that you are present as awareness. Again, see right at this moment that you are present *as awareness*. The beauty and simplicity of this fact cannot be overstated.

◆   If you are comfortable with the terms 'awakening' and 'liberation', that's fine. Only know that there is no **person** to awaken or to be liberated. Awakening is an **impersonal** occurrence, where the presence of awareness is recognized.

◆ Note that there is a spaciousness in which everything is happening. There may be a slew of thoughts, feelings, sounds and sensations occurring also. But if you carefully pause, you can discern a background of awareness that is, at once, vast, peaceful and ever-present. It is to that, ultimately, that Zen, Dzogchen, Advaita and the Tao are pointing.

◆   There is no way to come to this understanding through time. When a teacher tells you that it will take at least six weeks or six lifetimes for you to become self-realized, he or she is lying. Time and Being-ness are in no way related. **Being-ness is beyond time!** Indeed, one of the very first things you realize when you see this for yourself is the **immediacy** of presence. There is absolutely no separation from you and freedom itself.

◆   Indeed, you have never—for one moment—not been who you are.

◆ As a body-mind entity, you encounter three basic states of experience: waking, dreaming and deep sleep. But awareness is present in all three states. It is the substratum from which they arise. See it for yourself right now.

◆ You don't have to continually 're-awaken' and become 'identified' with awareness. Once this recognition or understanding happens, that's it. And it is there without cessation. And why shouldn't it, given that this is your natural and existing state?

◆ Non-duality is a systematic teaching that points to reality itself, which is nothing more than your ordinary, everyday awareness. Again, this is all that is being pointed to.

◆ In non-duality, we are not talking about a future or distant state. We are speaking about what you are at this very moment, *as you are reading these words*. You are the *presence* that is *aware* that these words are before you. Though your brain is processing them, it all comes back to presence as being the ultimate and unblinking witness. Thus, rather than attempting to be mindful of your thoughts and feelings, simply see that witnessing, in its ultimate form, is always *already* taking place.

◆ This understanding doesn't occur within the mind. The mind arises *in* it and can, in no way whatsoever, grasp or comprehend what surrounds it. All the mind does is respond to situations and perceptions, yielding thoughts, feelings and assessments that pale (totally) in capturing the limitlessness and wonder of our natural state.

◆ ***The mind is nothing but its contents***. You are the cognitizing spaciousness that knows that the contents are appearing.

◆ Spiritual stages are circumstantial, not cut in stone. With that said, the phases tend to be: ***suffering***, ***self-inquiry*** and ***awakening***. But self-knowledge can occur at any time, even without one having the slightest interest in non-duality. One can be waiting for a train, or picking up the morning paper, when suddenly, 'What the—'?

◆ Awareness is *already* present. Allow that fact to be with you throughout your day: Keep coming back to it, naturally and with total freshness. By 'freshness' I mean that you are genuinely paused by the re-appearance of the statement, that it seems new. Now stay with the pause, allowing it to reveal the fullness of its presence. ***What is it, right now, that would also be with you in deep sleep?***

◆ There are no awakenings on the level of 'body', 'mind' and 'soul'. That's just poppy-cock. Self-knowing occurs when a body-mind entity recognizes not only that it is present, but that it is present *as awareness*!

◆ Just because something is spiritual or spiritually sounding doesn't necessarily mean that it is an accurate pointer to your natural state. Does the phrase, comment or teaching directly point to what you are? If it doesn't pause you in any significant way, chances are it does not.

◆ What is spirituality? It is your essence, isn't it? It is your core being—that part of you that never changes. And the only thing about you that does not change is pure awareness. Thus, true spirituality automatically goes beyond any particular religion or denomination. See this for yourself so that it will be a living reality for you.

◆ One of the first things that anyone who has come to this understanding will tell you is, that awareness was there all the time. Not a single, truly awakened person will say to you, that self-realization requires virtues, practices, time, or meditation. The only people saying that are those who are not self-realized themselves and want you to hang onto them and their teachings.

◆ Awakening requires neither a 'facing' your fears nor a 'relinquishing' of your will or ego. There is a 'doer' in both those undertakings, and that 'doer' will automatically negate any substantive seeing or understanding from occurring. For your attention is still on this frequently appearing *practicality* ('I', 'me', 'you'), rather than on the *presence* within which the 'I', 'me', 'you' arises.

◆ *Awakening is not progressive*. As long as you are under that assumption, it will indeed be progressive. Why? Because you're giving credence to *time* being a factor in self-knowing, and it is not. Further, your progressive approach will never yield a final understanding, because you are inferring that, through your practices, you aren't awareness already. And nothing could be further from the truth.

◆ You are looking *away* from your Self.

◆ Awakening is the sudden seeing and understanding of what has always been present.

◆ Stay with what you are at this very moment. What is it that is currently being overlooked? It is a felt clarity that is without beginning or end.

◆ When you recognize your true self, you recognize the fundamental nature of the universe. Your apprehension is never less than that. So you can now see why this is sometimes called the *final* understanding. It is not that you stop learning. It's just that the essence of life is now known.

◆ You cannot help but 'be in the moment': The moment is all there is!

◆ There is nothing to be healed, awakened, or merged with. You *are* what you already are at this very moment. The felt presence of your ordinary, everyday awareness is the answer.

◆ There is absolutely no need for you to create some kind of 'psychological ground' (compassion, forgiveness, confession, poverty, celibacy, spiritual names, etc) for self-knowledge to occur. That's just a ploy that teachers and organizations use to get you to utilize their practices.

◆ You can't 'cultivate' what you already *are*. And just 'who' would be trying to do this anyway? It has to be some thought or notion telling you that you are not awareness itself, that you have to *attain* it. Can that temporary and woefully incorrect idea possibly be your fundamental identity?

◆ Something is already present. What is that 'something'?

◆ Everything arises spontaneously out of awareness. See that this is actually occurring in your daily life. Thoughts, emotions, sensations, consciousness and your body are *being known* by awareness. Bring your attention to this spacious knower that you heretofore have overlooked.

◆ Truth is not at the end of a road or journey. *It's right here and now, as you read these words*. The beginning is the end. Awareness recognized is all it is. You don't have to take a single step to anywhere to discover that. And the notion that you have to employ techniques or go on some sort of spiritual excursion is simply the mind holding sway. See your own immediate truth, and have a good laugh—or cry.

◆ *Q: I enjoy walking the mile or two for coffee in my not-quite-suburban, not-quite-rural edge of the city. The rhythm of one step in front of the other in the quiet morning allows a parade of thoughts and perceptions to stride by with equal ease.*

Rodney: That seeing of thoughts and perceptions 'with equal measure' is very good. It isn't something that you are *trying* to do. You are simply taking note of what is happening. You're the witness without attempting to be the witness. It sounds as if you're really starting to see how awareness 'presents' itself. I use the quotations, because awareness doesn't act, really. It is simply ever-present. Your recognition of it **appears** to come from you because, as a sentient being, you have the ability to know not only that you exist, but that you exist—fundamentally—**as awareness itself**, and not just as a body and a mind.

Q: That is evident right now. Here I am, the individual moving through a scene; yet, the whole scene is also within me. Then, there is the true me—the stillness that encompasses the whole scene, with the perception of time ticking with each step within this eternity of now.

Rodney: Right, the stillness is the seer. The witnessing is coming from that. You are the spaciousness in which all of those things are occurring. There isn't this defined 'I' within you that is continually 'doing' the seeing, the knowing. The 'I' is occasional, so it can't possibly be the knower. **The knower has to be something that never changes**. So just bring your attention to your ordinary, everyday awareness. See the peace and spaciousness with which it is magnificently imbued. Don't be overly concerned about the witnessing. It will take care of itself, as it has always done! Just remain with the fundamental issue: What is it about yourself, right at this moment, that never moves from what it is? That is the question to deliberate upon, to be totally paused by.

Q: *Exactly. You once told me that 'whatever makes you stop' is all it takes. I am fully witnessing that thought right now, as I am filled with gratitude by my noticing what is always here—this non-dual reality. Thank you for offering me those words. They make all of this so clear and easy.*

Rodney: You're most welcome. Your own beginningless Self is right there, right now. Whatever you are doing, you are looking at and through it at this very moment. It never moves from being fully available, and its recognition is just a matter of noticing that, during a pause in thinking or feeling, there is an immeasurable presence of awareness **that has always been there**. We are merely distracted by a rising thought or emotion. But the truth of the matter is, we never move from this. We absolutely never do.

◆   The ego is just the **sense** of an individual self. It is not an **actual** thing or division.

◆   Presence is looking at itself through this body's eyes. That this body happens to be named Rodney, is male, is tall and loves dark chocolate, is purely circumstantial. There is nothing here but presence. Everything is coming up from and disappearing into That.

◆ Your body does not have a life of its own. It is composed of and is animated by presence. Thus, you are *being* lived. ***There is no separate person living a life***. You are a wave on the ocean and are nothing but water itself.

◆ Existence is simply awareness finding expression in infinite forms and actions.

◆ Awareness isn't something that is merely constantly present. It is what you *are*. So stop trying to *gain* or *reach* for presence. You are looking *beyond* it, so to speak, when you attempt to do that. So what is it, right at this moment, that you cannot look beyond? *That* is who and what you are! *That* is your heart and treasure. See what is 'doing' the seeing and the knowing—It is that seemingly ordinary spaciousness that is directly before and within you. And truly, it couldn't be any simpler to recognize.

◆ No matter what is happening, you are looking into awareness at that very moment.

◆ Though you may shed a tear or burst out laughing, awakening is not an emotional issue. Also, whether you're a compassionate person or a callous one, it is not a factor when it comes to perceiving your natural state.

◆ There can be no collective understanding of the natural state. It happens to one person at a time. And though it is a relatively rare and singular event, that is only because of the ease with which presence can be overlooked, and not because it is difficult to understand or because it is a time-related issue.

◆ In a magazine article I came across the line, 'However, by practising awareness, we can train ourselves...' But how can you 'practise' what you already *are*? The notion is ludicrous. And *who* is this separate entity or person that is going to be 'trained' into seeing awareness? Again, it's all meditative gobbledygook.

◆ Meditation only strengthens the notion that there is a person there, and not presence.

◆ Methods and techniques remain peripheral. Self-enquiry and earnest deliberation do not.

◆ In regards to non-duality, getting 'in touch with your feelings' is a massive waste of time. You are what you are at this very moment, regardless of what you are thinking or feeling. See the power and immediate reality of this. You are what you are *at this very moment*, regardless of what you're thinking or feeling.

◆   If you are genuinely interested in knowing your natural state, then 'freeing' yourself of everyday thoughts, emotions and actions is not the way to go about it. Instead, go to the source—presence itself. Then other matters will take care of themselves.

◆   You can't 'rest' or 'abide' in the natural state. That would be someone *in addition* to the state itself.

◆   Don't dismiss small insights. They could lead to larger and more potent ones. Besides, if you give your full attention to the pause and stillness *after* any insight, you can immediately know and discern absolute freedom.

◆   You can't use meditation to 'get beyond the mind'. Why not? Because you are expressly using the mind when you are meditating! However, seeing the bare truth of this statement *does* point you beyond any imagined thinker or meditator.

◆   A thought cannot be aware of awareness. So what is it that is aware of the thought?

◆   The mind is not composed of thoughts: 'Mind' *is* a thought. When the thought disappears, so does the mind.

◆ In your natural state, peace *is* the spacious; and the spaciousness, peace. One blends into the other and never becomes wholly defined. There is no movement and yet, this non-state is alive, knowing and wondrous. It is your bright, true self, without a single limitation.

◆ People who put emphasis on 'the path' to awakening do so, because, in their heart of hearts, they do not believe that this can happen to them. So they give themselves an out by going on and on about the importance of 'the journey' rather than the destination. But true enlightenment (if you want to use that word) is a sudden discovery that you are *already* 'located' at the very place to which you are attempting to journey. So just sit with this for a few moments—or however much time you feel comfortable giving it. See the reality of your situation. That reality is merely being *overlooked*— that's all. It is as simple as that.

◆ Meditation and mindfulness are merely *thinking* about those activities. You never move from the mental and conceptual realms when you engage in either of those undertakings.

◆ My body is temporarily here. But *whose* body is it? It's not my body, really. Does the wave in the ocean own itself?

◆ Though you may have aged, what is it that has *not* changed? Contemplate this as you read these words. What is it that has not altered in the least? And remember, it can't be consciousness, because consciousness changes (you sleep, wake, dream, etc). So what is it that, unequivocally, has not moved?

◆ The primary cause of sorrow is not our grasping for happiness, but our identification with the mind, body and sensations. We try to find lasting happiness through each of them every single day, and we can't, because each is constantly changing. Yet, we continue to give them our every hope. You are that which is *aware* of your body, thoughts and sensations. You are awareness itself—which is directly in front of you.

◆ The recognition of truth doesn't take place over time. Presence is suddenly seen or discerned, and that's the end of it. However, your body mind's *experience* with this understanding will occur over the apparentness of time, as your life is being lived. But self-knowledge itself is not gradual, and any teaching that says so is false.

◆ Awakening is a sudden seeing of what you truly **are**. The 'who' remains, but it is merely functional. This 'I' allows us to communicate and go about our daily lives. After all, there are still errands to be run, conversations to be had and laundry to be done. But your personality pretty much remains as it is, though thoughts and reactions have far less weight now.

◆ You see, it's okay for the thinker to come to an end— because it was never there in the first place. So don't fear or envision that, with self knowledge, you will be 'losing' some precious something. Thinking will continue. It's just that thoughts won't unnecessarily be linked together into some defined or imagined whole.

◆ Self-realization is simply being aware of yourself as you naturally are. You are seeing, essentially, that you are a **what**, not a **who**. The 'who' is merely a wave on the water—undeniably unique and present (at least temporarily), but water nonetheless.

◆ Once the mind pauses, true creativity occurs. Thought comes afterwards, with a response or assessment of that particular piece of writing, music, painting, artwork, singing, dancing, knitting, basket weaving, scientific theorizing, etc.

◆   The universe has no purpose for existing. And neither do you. But as long as you believe that you are your body and your mind, a wise move might be to understand why you are neither of the above, and have never been.

◆   In truth, you are Existence itself. Your seeming individuality is a temporary and occasional occurrence that arises out of awareness proper.

◆   Many seekers point to their being decade-plus meditators with enormous pride. But what is there to be proud of? You have been ignoring the obvious the entire time. And even if you were to label yourself as an 'accomplished' meditator, you are still a meditator. There is still this imagined individual there. Why not bring your attention to the source of these manifestations, a source that is subtle, eternal and magnificent? Indeed, it is meditation itself!

◆   When I am pointing to presence, I am pointing to **you**—not to something far off or slightly to the left or right of you. I'm pointing to **what** you are at this very moment.

◆   You are what you are right here and now. See that there is a very definite **presence of awareness** within and before you as you peruse these words. Just sit with this, ponder it, and allow for an easy and very natural discerning of your fundamental state.

◆ Your focus is wrongly placed on the mind. Bring your attention to awareness, which you are merely overlooking. Besides, there is no transformation of the mind in self-realization—never has been and never will be. Books and teachers who claim otherwise are unconditionally wrong.

◆ Throughout the day, try refusing—in a safe and responsible manner—to play along with occasional thoughts, feelings and sentiments. You may be surprised to find how much clarity and energy you have towards the evening. Don't make this into a practice. It is just a revealing exploration of the workings of your mind and persona.

◆ You don't have to **halt** your thinking to discover truth. Just note that there is a natural spaciousness **between** each thought. And it is within that spaciousness that the Ultimate can be discerned.

◆ Many seekers give an aliveness to the mind that simply isn't there. They claim that it wants nothing but power or that it orchestrates cunning ways to defeat your attempts to suppress it. But the mind is nothing but the arising and disappearing of thoughts, concepts and feelings. There is no defined 'thing' present. You are the pauses **between** the thoughts!

◆ Awareness is self-luminous and without beginning or end. And you are That. What is it, within you, that has those qualities or attributes? See for yourself That which has always been readily apparent.

◆ There is no bridge to truth. You are *already* on the other side.

◆ *This is key: You exist as awareness*. Your body, thoughts and sensations are appearances *in* that awareness.

◆ *No separate objects are ever witnessed—only awareness*.

◆ When you meditate, you think you are accomplishing something, but you aren't. It is just a massive waste of time, energy and money (if payment or expenses are involved). Why are you attempting to be something that you already *are*? Where is the logic in that? Or the sanity? And because self-knowing does not transpire in that manner, you are going to spend a lifetime striving to 'achieve' something that absolutely will not occur!

◆ 'Enlightenment' is not an 'empty mind'. Rather, it is the teeming presence of awareness in which the so-called mind sporadically arises.

◆ So much spiritual writing is pure fluff. And that fluff is not going to help you in the least to recognize your fundamental state. It may make for entertaining reading or workshops, but it will not pause your thinking in any significant or life-changing way.

◆ Life goes on quite nicely without this imagined 'you' of yours. Aliveness, richness and spontaneity are the very nature of living. And you *are* that Livingness. You are giving undue attention to a sporadic appearance (the ego) instead of to the majestic course of existence itself.

◆ Non-duality is not the transformation of anything (especially oneself). It is the *seeing* or *understanding* of a *presence* that has *always* been in place.

◆ Awareness is *always* 'choiceless': You don't have to practise to make it so. You will only be getting in the way of something that is already incomprehensibly pristine.

◆ There is blessedly little spiritual drama in non-duality. There are no *sannyasins* in some fiery state of concentration, desperately attempting to burn away the last vestiges of the ego. But, as I keep saying here, the only time the ego will be dead is when you are dead. Just see *through* the ego (i.e. that it is merely a momentary arising of a sense of individuality) and it's no longer a problem.

◆ Just to be clear: There is no one to 'let go' of anything. What happens is that a thought or notion or sentiment comes up. And if you don't like it, you say, 'I've got to let go of that'. That sentence is just another thought. No defined 'me' has been created. Nor was there ever one.

◆ You are fixated on this spiritual mirage of 'enlightenment', and of it being ecstatic and rife with visions and spirals of energy cruising throughout your body. But self-knowledge is none of those things. In fact, it's not even 'spiritual' in its purest sense. We are talking about a very natural state—of peace and limitlessness— that is simply not being noticed.

◆ 'Strengthening your spirit', 'awakening the mind' and 'expanding your awareness' are just catch-phrases for doing nothing at all. They sound like spiritually important endeavours, but they aren't. In fact, they are ludicrous. The recognition of your natural condition requires none of the above.

◆ Two spiritual myths: Awakening is *not* the product of personal growth; and awareness does *not* need to be 'expanded'. Indeed, awareness is freedom and spaciousness itself! It is completely without bounds, and it is precisely what you are. Hence, there is nothing whatsoever that is personal about it.

◆ As long as you are focusing at the level of cause and effect, you will likely never discern That which is unequivocally beyond it.

◆ Self-knowledge is not a process. It is an end in itself. It is the abandonment of all rituals, practices and *sadhanas*. It is the simple seeing of your unalloyed Self.

◆ All practices are extraneous and distracting. I'm almost tempted to say comical, as well. But it's more a feeling of sadness that comes up here. For most seekers are truly well-meaning folks. They want nothing more than 'enlightenment' itself. But they think—because of erroneous books and clueless teachers—that awakening is progressive and time-laden. And nothing could be further from the truth.

◆ *There are no answers outside of yourself.*

◆ Self-realization is the simple recognition of who and what you are. That recognition is neither time-dependent nor place-dependent. Neither is it contingent upon your being silent or still—though you may be momentarily paused or quiet when the understanding occurs.

◆ Give minimal attention to any so-called spiritual experience. That, in itself, will spare you lots of lost time, misdirection and needless investigation.

◆ What is it, right now, that is absolutely *not* changing?

◆ You cannot force or will self-knowledge into existence. It is a seeing or understanding of what is already fully present. No efforts are needed, except the easy contemplation of the words that you are reading right now.

◆ With the practice of meditation and mindfulness, you are saying that you are something *other* than awareness, and that you must somehow work your way *towards* that notion or idea. And thus misery ensues, because a concept cannot be attained.

◆ Why divide things into 'spiritual' and 'material'? Simply enjoy life as best you can—especially when it comes to opportunities to spend time in nature or with good-hearted people, or simply by yourself at a corner table in a cafe or coffee shop, watching the rain fall or reading an insightful book.

◆ Don't attempt to *be* quiet. Just see that there is a quietness *already* within you. And there is never a moment when you are without it.

◆ Contemplation and self-reflection are important in non-duality. They happen best when you deliberate over some point in a relaxed and natural manner. And remember, you're not looking for an *intellectual* understanding to this, but for an actual *presence* of awareness that is both boundless and unchanging.

◆ Why do you want to be 'on the road' to happiness? The actual state of things is that sometimes you're happy and sometimes you are not. There is no place where happiness is constant. For happiness is an *experience*, and it is the very nature of experiences to change. Awareness, however, is your natural state. It is consummate and unvarying.

◆ Your Self is *already* centred. There is nothing wayward about it at all. If it were, it wouldn't be the Self! And it is manifesting itself in you right now as a subtle but irrefutable *presence* of *peace* and *pervasiveness*.

◆ Anger, uncertainty, bitterness, impatience, a broken heart, etc are all things that can naturally come up in the body-mind. Why does there need to be 'someone' who 'stays with' any of those arisings? Such an action would only increase the duration of that particular emotion, because you're *re*-focusing on it—and, with an imagined witness added to it, no less! Just let the feelings be, as long as there is no harm to you or anyone. Besides, do you *attempt* to witness feelings of love, joy, pleasure, gratitude and compassion? No! You simply allow them to have their times and moments in your life. And then they disappear.

◆ *There is literally no boundary to who and what you are*.

◆ Presence is one of the things you are seeing right at the moment. You just aren't noticing it. You are certainly aware of your bodily sensations and your sporadic thoughts and feelings. Ditto any sounds that may be occurring. But come back to awareness by taking note of what it is—right here and now—that you are looking *beyond*.

◆ See that awareness is the only thing that is *continually* before you. *It Does Not Move*. What is it, right now, that is ever the same?

◆ This understanding is not a matter of 'personal growth'. It is about the ultimate truth of your existence. Therefore, it will never be very popular, because seekers want to drag their imagined selves along and make a 'spiritual journey' out of self-knowing. In short, they want to romanticize it. But all that is required is a relaxed kind of seeing, a focusing.

◆ Buddha kept pointing out 'the illusion of the self'. And that's a good thing. For it's because of that illusion that you feel that you must *do* something to *attain* something. But given that there is neither a 'doer' thereof nor a hair's breadth of separation between you and presence, methods and practices are completely unnecessary. Indeed, they *prevent* you from seeing what was never lost!

◆ You *are* awareness! Why do you need to move from that?

◆   You just cannot be 'permanently free of mind identification'—unless you're dead! Don't believe popular writers and speakers who tell you this. Brief identification with thoughts and feelings still sporadically occurs with self-realization. But that identification disappears just as quickly as it arises. It is like going to the cinema: You know it's a movie, yet you sometimes get caught up in the story. You laugh about it after the show. You may even have substantive discussions about the film with good friends. Knowing your fundamental nature is far more important than any fleeting identification with a passing thought or emotion.

◆   Does a thought know that you are experiencing it? What, then, is doing the knowing?... Don't move from this... **What**, then, is doing the knowing?

◆   This understanding is **not** a transformational process! Nothing really happens, except a full and sudden knowing of that which is subtle and yet magnificent. Your day goes on as before, but now with an unalloyed vastness behind all of that arises. The immenseness was always there, of course—unhidden and being exactly what it is.

◆   Awakening (enlightenment, self-realization, etc) doesn't 'mature'. You can certainly garner experience with being awake. But your natural state remains ever the same.

◆ The mind doesn't need to be brought into harmony with presence. (Would you be capable of doing that anyway?) All that is needed is a clear seeing that your so-called mind is not a thing unto itself, but rather, the mere ascending of thoughts, images and concepts *within* a spaciousness to which you have given scant attention.

◆ You say that you 'welcome everything into being'. But who is doing the welcoming? *Who*, precisely, is at the door, motioning for everything to come in? Even awareness doesn't 'welcome' manifestation. It simply *knows* that a specific something has appeared. Return to what you *are*—unbounded presence and clarity—by noticing what is *directly* within and before you.

◆ You disappear into the Absolute after every thought and emotion. Why, then, strive to do this as a method or practice? And *who* would be the entity that would be attempting to do this? In such spiritual endeavours, you are simply getting in the way of yourself.

◆ Any form of spiritual gradualness is simply the mind in full operation.

◆ 'How do I attain enlightenment?' is the wrong question. It's the wrong question, because your ideas about enlightenment are incorrect. Also, enlightenment, per se, does not exist. So these false notions about the issue are distracting you from seeing what is directly in front of you. Thus, a far better question would be: 'What is the presence of awareness that is cognizing my body and thinking right here and now?'

◆ Meditation can give you some calmness—but never peace which only comes with the recognition of your natural state. Meditation isn't natural. It's an endeavour that has to be done again and again and again. Self-realization, on the other hand, happens only once. Boom! Game over.

◆ You are not your body, thoughts and emotions. They are certainly there, but there has to be something that **knows** that they are there, and you **are** that something—awareness itself. And you can't get more liberated than that!

◆ However poetic it sounds, the 'dissolution of the ego' is a meaningless and non-ending aspiration. Any teacher who has you doing that is just wasting your time and money. The ego, which is just another thought, is going to continue to come up (and disappear) as long as your body is being lived. Why not **investigate the assumed reality of the person** who is attempting to get rid of the ego?

34

◆ Go beyond any feelings of goodness or happiness or sadness or even bliss. Even the universe depends upon *your* existence! You are Supreme Reality. How is it, that you could ever be separate from That which is without beginning or end?

◆ You are Pure Being itself. Nothing in the universe can excel you.

◆ This understanding happens during a pause in your thinking. So any attempts to 'reach' reality through memorization or theorizing or recitation will simply not succeed. For those actions are just further forms of conceptualization.

◆ *You are not an object*. Anything that comes up, changes and/or disappears can't possibly be you. Sort through the potency and pointing within those words and discover their truth for yourself. For that's where the answer lies: Your own innate peace and limitlessness.

◆ There are numerous ways in which you can come to this understanding: Direct recognition, inference, pointers, ordinary daily events etc. But every single one of those things involves *a pause*. It is key to this whole dynamic (or non-dynamic) of self-knowing. And the pause should happen naturally. *You* do not instigate it. In fact, you will clearly see that there is no 'you' to initiate it. It just happens. The important thing to note is that the pause is occurring, and that the pause is presence itself. Again, *the pause is presence itself*. There are no steps here—just a hushed and placid suddenness to the entire recognition.

◆ Our so-called 'minds' are *dis*-continuous, but awareness is not. Look for that which never changes.

◆ It's utterly foolish to try to 'negate' the ego. For the negating itself is a mental process. So nothing can come of it, except frustration. You are the spaciousness in which those thoughts and processes are occurring. Stay with what you *are*. Stay with the Vastness-That-Does-Not-Move.

◆ Truly, the simplicity of this is (quite literally) *beyond* belief.

◆ Lasting happiness can only be found with that which is lasting. And that is *presence*, which is even greater than happiness, given that happiness is a condition that is variable.

◆ Emotion has very little to do with this understanding. That's why any strivings to attain it through love, compassion and doing good works is a recipe for failure. The previously mentioned qualities come about naturally and spontaneously once you are clear about your fundamental nature. So allow your focus to be on self-knowledge itself, rather than on the means—however exemplary—to garner it.

◆ If you are having numerous 'awakenings' and 'realizations', you haven't awakened. You are simply having *experiences* which—despite the spiritual myth—are *not* steppingstones to self-knowing. I say this not to be critical, but to point out a truth. You are That which is *beyond* all experiences. So why do yourself such a disservice by seeking and revelling in them?

◆   Your identification with your body and thinking is distracting you from discovering your glorious and fundamental nature. That identification can't be stopped conceptually, ritualistically, philosophically or ceremonially. Indeed, the whole issue of your understanding who and what you are is not an overwhelmingly spiritual one. We couch it in those terms because, historically, we have associated the numinous and the indescribable with the theological. Only those clear-seeing sages of non-dual lore—from Gaudapada and Shankara to Nisargadatta and Sailor Bob Adamson—have pointed *directly* to our natural and pristine state rather than heavenward. And that state is there for *seeing*. Just bring your calm attention to that subtle peace and freedom that is fully within you, right *here* and *now*.

◆   You are that which is *aware* of your body, feelings and thinking.

◆   Questions related to self-knowledge are raised by the so-called mind in consciousness. But such questions cannot be answered by the mind. For the answer is not a word or an action. Nor is it an experience. Rather, it is your own ever-existing *presence* of equanimity and spaciousness.

◆   Awareness... In its obviousness, we miss it.

◆ 'You are sitting: You are **aware** that you are sitting: You **are** that awareness.' That's the only 'guided meditation' (which it isn't) that you need ever use. As for all the other GM rubbish about *chakras*, planes, *mudras*, anchoring, observing the breath, and the particularly hallowed and ubiquitous 'Just let it go', I say, just let them go.

◆ You can only recognize presence in the waking state, because consciousness is needed to perceive awareness. So what is it, right now, that would also be with you in deep sleep, even if you weren't conscious that it was present?

◆ Self-inquiry isn't something that you have to work at. It comes up naturally and on its own, when the '**Who?**' question arises throughout the day ('**Who** wants to witness his thoughts?' '**Who** wants to better control his emotions?' etc). The question, if unprompted and spontaneous, truly pauses you. And in that halting, felt awareness can be readily perceived. In short, you will see that the pause is the answer.

◆ Don't get caught up in the 'witnessing position'. If you do, you can easily remain there for the rest of your days. And it will all be for naught, for the witness that you are attempting to utilize is only an apparent one, a phantom that isn't able to help you to see anything. Further, witnessing is *already* being done by awareness anyway, which is your true and limitless Self.

◆ You struggle to 'attain' awareness when, in actuality, there is no way *out* of it.

◆ How can there be steps and practices to what you already *are*? Take a moment to see and feel the significance of that question. What is it, right now, that is subtly (yet fully) present and that does not change?

◆ One of your problems is that you are looking for a state that is blissful. And you will no doubt find it, if you search, struggle and sacrifice long enough. But such experiences won't last. Why? Because your *real* nature is peace and spaciousness, which are eternal and do not disappoint.

◆ You are that Ultimate Oneness at this very second. Consciousness, the world, the colossal oceans and all the universe are effortlessly contained within you—again, *at this very moment*. We are not philosophizing here or proposing psychological theories or prophesying—just pointing to a simple and very evident truth.

◆ Right here and now, you are your own *dharma*, your own 'right path'. Nothing is needed except a clear and immediate seeing that you are That—awareness itself. You are simply being led by your mind and your imagination when you attempt to search for truth through spiritual journeys, prolonged concentration and ascetic practices. You are your own *dharma*, your own 'right path'. Stay with the beauty of your natural and eternal presence. And what could be more effortless than that?

◆ Presence is the most marvellous thing. See and recognize it for yourself. Nothing, I assure you, could be easier or simpler. And why would it not? You **are** That!

◆ *Nirvana* is a beautiful Sanskrit word that originally means 'to blow out' or 'putting out fire'. This definition is apt because with self-realization comes the exquisite absence of any burning desires or cravings for anything or anyone. Nothing outmeasures the sereneness that you feel within you. It is, at once, profound, unwavering and complete.

◆ Always be mindful of the fact that awareness isn't being concealed ever. Neither is it something that you have to acquire or work toward. It is simply being **overlooked**. The more you give heed to this truth, the sooner you will come to see your own irrefutable reality.

◆ The mind can never grasp reality. That understanding occurs when the mind stops, such as during breaks in thoughts or when there is a pause due to some pointing or pondering. But during those times, we really aren't brought any 'closer' to what we are. For we never move from this Reality. It's just that during pauses and deep reflecting our seeing is clearer, less foggy, and free of distractions.

◆ Your dual consciousness will remain only as long as you are living. But there is nothing eternal about it, so it can't possibly be your fundamental reality.

◆ Thoughts, feelings, emotions, ideas and images are *not* you. They are simply *arisings* in the immeasurableness that *is* you. And you never cease being this, so there is no need for you to strive to 'reach' or 'attain' it. But most seekers are trying to 'conquer' presence, so that they can exclaim that they have done so and then point to the travails that they have endured in order to acquire it. But the irony is that they will never reach it that way. They will, however, experience any number of sensations, manifestations and conditions. So at least they can take 'consolation' in that!

◆ Always be mindful of the point that something is being **overlooked**. That's all. There is unequivocally nothing to be 'merged' with or to become 'established' in. That kind of spiritual drivel will keep you in conceptual whorls for the rest of your days, which would be tragic, given that not only are you already free, you are Freedom itself!

◆ Self-knowing isn't 'being connected to' or 'being at one with' some larger reality. It is recognizing that you are presence proper—that there is no division or distance from that for which you are seeking. Coming to this understanding can appear as a thunderbolt or as an eventless occurrence (more often the latter). Every personality is different. But the understanding is the same.

◆ The answer that you're looking for is **spaciousness**. It is neither an experience nor anything that can be experienced. Again, the answer that you are searching for is bare, utter spaciousness. You're looking through it and into it **right here and now**, as you read these words. Feel yourself being paused by what is blazingly before and within you at this very moment.

◆ *Existence is the manifested aspect of the Unmanifested: One is simply the other. Names, labels and distinctions come up as thoughts and images in our so-called minds. Otherwise, no distinctions are present.*

◆   The mystique of 'enlightenment' induces you not only to overlook awareness proper, but to pursue spiritual experiences and imagined visions in the hope of attaining some sort of dramatic truth. But the full measure of what you are is already right before you, and it is subtle, boundless and unchanging. It is peace itself.

◆   If you have the opportunity to speak and be with someone for whom this is a living reality, take advantage of that opportunity. You may not come away with any immediate understanding (and then again, you just might), but at least the pointing will be consistent and spot-on. And there will be no wavering or half-measures—the truth will be fully articulated.

◆   No 'I-thought' or 'ego' can be 'awakened'. When the transient nature of these things is clearly seen, presence naturally and very obviously remains.

◆   *The purpose of non-duality is not to reach some imagined or mythical state, but to clarify your identity*. And this clarification or understanding isn't difficult or time-dependent in the least. It is a simple seeing of what is immediately before you. It is that which is present *before* your next thought, feeling or doubt arises.

◆ Ponder the following question: Your thoughts arise—*in what*?... Notice that there is a pause directly after the question. But you are **overlooking** the pause, because you think that is just an ordinary emptiness there, rather than a vastness that is rich with love and equanimity. Take a moment to see yourself as your Self. And perhaps you too will be exclaiming J.W. Work's enduring spiritual lyrics, 'Free at last, Free at last! Thank God Almighty I'm free at last!'

◆ Because the 'I' and 'me' repeatedly come up throughout the day, we assume that there is a separate person present. But **repetition doesn't necessarily infer Essence**. What is it that does **not** arise and disappear? That is your treasure.

◆ Self-inquiry fails for most seekers, because they attempt to inquire into **who** they are, instead of into the **what-ness** of their existence. And this **what-ness** appears to us as utter peace and spaciousness. It is without beginning or end, and no terms, concepts and descriptions can't even begin to capture its fullness and fragrance.

◆ Apperceiving means seeing through the formations of the 'I' with such clarity, that your thinking is halted, and you find yourself as presence itself. It is both a new understanding and a final one.

◆   Be the witness? You already *are* the witness! Who is this added watcher that you are bringing into the equation? If you examine the issue carefully, you will see that this appended 'me' is just a thought or idea *about* who you are. It is *not* Self itself. It is not the *what-ness* of your existence.

◆   Understanding leads to direct, natural, and even intuitive actions. There is no person present during such activity, just the actions and responses themselves, in the full sweep of life.

◆   The richness and spaciousness within seekers is *overlooked* largely because their attention is given to their thoughts, practices and seeking, rather than to awareness proper. Such seekers are attempting to 'attain' awareness, rather than simply *recognizing* it.

◆   The first step of ninety-nine percent of all meditators is to focus on the mind (or some aspect of it). Then they attempt to either control what is there or to witness it. But any attempts to 'tame' the mind or to add yet another 'perceiver' to Reality will, by default, only lead you to a lifetime of striving and disappointment. And by focusing, in the very first instance, on the mind is a supreme error. Your focus should be on *presence*, and how your feelings, self-concepts, and even consciousness, arise *within* it.

46

◆ All questions and paradoxes are dissolved with Knowledge.

◆ You can come to a direct knowing of what you are by either recognizing this subtle yet penetrating *presence of awareness* that is squarely before you, or by you thoroughly and suddenly understanding that the 'I', 'me', and even sentience (your knowing that you exist) *has* to arise *within* something that is *already* present.

◆ In progressive paths, you are trying to utilize the 'I' (a frequent yet fleeting appearance *in* awareness) to *reach* awareness. The foolishness of such an endeavour should be immediately evident.

◆ God is not something to be feared or periodically 'communed' with. God is always with you and *as* you. He/She/It is that indescribable tranquillity and vastness that remains after seeing through the falseness of self-centred concepts. And this isn't a case of your having to take various issues—love, lust, suffering, envy, faith, the mind, etc—and examine them separately in some structured and in-depth manner. That's a concept ('me') attempting to examine another concept. Presence, however, dispels all illusions with wholeness and radiance.

◆ Awareness is *prior* to any thought, doubt, seeking or spiritual exercise.

47

◆ There has never been any separation between you and presence. As you are reading these words right now, you **are** the very truth that you are seeking. Ponder this over and over again, if you feel so inclined. And there must be a natural proclivity to do so; otherwise, it is purely a conceptual endeavour.

◆ Happiness isn't our inherent nature. Peace is.

◆ All journeys, however contemplative, take you in the wrong direction. Journeys are a pull for you, because they promise drama, suspense, romance, and difficulties (to be bravely surmounted). You cannot make a journey without taking your 'self' along. And this imagined 'me' is what keeps all of your illusions alive. Before taking any step in any direction, sit down and reflect upon what it is that is currently within you—but is **not** a thought, a sensation or an emotion.

◆ You can't come to this understanding through stages. Neither are there any 'gradual dissolutions', 'speedy unfoldings', or 'dark nights of the soul'. Awakening, for the lack of a better word, is sudden and complete. And with it comes the knowledge that, in no uncertain terms, **there is no separation between the perceiver and the perceived**, and that **all divisions in life are only apparent**. In short, awareness has already 'happened'! Take a non-moment to see what you are **over**-looking, and not what you need to strive for or attain.

48

◆ Why get bent out of shape about duality? It is simply an appearance *in* Reality. Objects, lives and occurrences are manifestations, giving rise to the concepts of space and time. Beyond and within all of this is *a timelessness* that defies all description. And you *are* that! There is not the slightest separation between you and awareness. Ponder this fact throughout day and evening, until you are suddenly clear on its magnificent reality.

◆ The mind is not a distinct entity. Rather, it is a *functioning* that occurs within the brain. And that functioning includes thinking, feeling, intending, guessing, reasoning and imagining.

◆ Consciousness, among other things, is the *sense* of existing and the *sense* of being present. There is an 'I am-ness' quality to consciousness that is not there with awareness. As a sentient being, you know that you exist, that you are sitting, right now, directly in front of your computer screen, as you peruse these sentences. But when you are awake to your actual nature, you not only know that you exist, but that you are Existence *Itself*.

◆ Sentience/consciousness is an aspect of awareness that allows awareness to recognize itself. Pure non-dual presence, which you ultimately are, does not know that it exists.

◆   There is really no 'relationship' between awareness and the universe. Such topics may (seemingly) make for entertaining debates with a lot of weighted—but not necessarily correct—conjecture. But the bottom line is that awareness and all worlds are one. No matter the distance, the dimension or the condition—*all* is presence.

◆   Your un-examined, day-to-day living amounts to your taking yourself to be something that you are not.

◆   One of the great myths of enlightenment (which is another myth in itself) is that, upon its occurrence, all notions of dualism cease. There still may be the occasional—but brief—identification with thoughts and feelings. But essentially, your life becomes rather like a lucid dream: You know that you are dreaming, but you still react to the sudden and oncoming bus, or return a beautiful person's smile and gaze. But all is seen for what it is: temporary appearances *within* the dream. So ultimately nothing is held, only enjoyed, steered clear of, or reacted to normally.

◆   There is no road to freedom, only Freedom itself.

◆   'Deepening' your practice accomplishes nothing. It is still a practice and there is still this 'perceived person' doing it. Further, at no point do you 'reach' presence, because it can only be recognized or understood, *not attained*. In short, with methods and practices, you are looking *away* from the very thing that you are seeking.

◆   Without a single belief or a nanosecond of any spiritual activity, awareness gleams radiantly before you. And it isn't so much because you are distracted by life that you aren't seeing it (though that contention is not without merit): You just haven't properly paused and cognitized the *presence* of awareness within that pause. And such a recognition comes simply and easily.

◆   Awakening is a direct understanding of your true nature. And it occurs only once—and that's it. Game over.

◆   You are aware of these words as you are reading them on the computer screen. But *what* is it that is aware? Pause carefully here. What is it that is immediately present *in addition to* the words that you are reading right now? See that there is a subtle *presence* of sheerness and spaciousness that has absolutely always been within you and before you. It is the Mona Lisa smile within the 3D picture. It may appear hidden at first, but once perceived, you realize how it was always in rapturous view.

◆ The 'I' is a convenience, a practicality, an assumed reference point that allows us to function and communicate in our day-to-day life. Attempt neither to negate it or to give it overwhelming importance. For your fundamental nature can't be anything that comes and goes. And the 'I' and the 'me' do just that. You are the splendour and the spaciousness that forever remains.

◆ Just see or understand that you are **presence**, first and foremost. ***There is no extra entity having to remain 'focused' on anything***. Then you will quickly discern that this peace and clarity doesn't come and go. They remain because they are authentic aspects of your Beingness. You continue to experience emotions (thank goodness!), but they are seen for what they are: fleeting arisings in your natural state.

◆ You are completely wasting your time, if you are attempting to end or dissolve the ego. That is simply one thought or concept trying to negate another. And the harder and longer you try, the more frustrating it will become. Is that any way to live your life, especially a so-called spiritual one?

◆   The issue with recognizing presence is not so much its *subtlety* (though that is certainly a factor), but its *immediacy*. Even *before* you begin to sit in meditation or pick up a spiritual book or read the next word in this very sentence, your natural state is brilliantly present.

◆   True awakening doesn't cause 'disorientation'. Indeed, you are suddenly centred in ways that you could not imagine. And it's little wonder, given that you are then *centredness*, i.e. *awareness proper*. You were that even before your awakening, of course, but now you know it to be actual.

◆   There is no need for you to 're-examine certain patterns of thinking' or create some sort of 'energetic unfolding'. Those are conceptual activities that never go beyond their self-perpetuating little loops.

◆   Awakening *ends* the process of seeking. If you're still meditating and going to your teacher for counsel, you have not recognized anything.

◆　　There is no separation between you and awareness. Ponder this, naturally and earnestly. Truly let it sink in. Again, *there is absolutely no separation between you and awareness*. If there is any grand or root precept to non-duality, that's the one. You *are* this knowing, unblinking spaciousness that is within and before your so-called body and mind. Indeed, there is no way out, really. So why not stop all the struggling and take a non-moment to recognize this unabashed refulgence that you have continually been overlooking?

◆　　Consciousness is local. Awareness is *non*-local.

◆　　The 'new awakening' is the old awakening. Or rather, there is nothing new or old about it. It is timeless and beyond all categorizations. Why some writers and gurus attempt to make this understanding into something contemporary is puzzling.

◆　　There is no 'expansion' of awareness when it is recognized. That is one of those ridiculous notions put forward by teachers who have no clarity about themselves or non-duality. When true understanding occurs, awareness is seen as expansiveness itself. It is a sheerness that is completely without bounds. Even to talk of expansion and expansiveness when it comes to presence is to short-change it in an almost laughable way.

◆ More often than not, meditation doesn't quiet the mind. Rather, it tends to make thoughts more apparent. Why? Because all of your attention is on stopping the thoughts. And when that happens, you are prone to be *more* aware when any thought appears. Even when you say that you are simply 'witnessing the thought' or 'just letting thoughts come and go', there is this imagined person there, attempting to do either thing. So you still haven't gotten any closer to who and what you truly are. You can easily go a lifetime in this nonsensical loop, and—of course—most meditators do.

◆ Can love and devotion really be practised? Or are they simply a spontaneous and unbridled outpouring from the heart? This is one of those spiritual questions for which the answer can be readily intuited, even if it cannot yet be clearly seen.

◆ Self-inquiry is beyond 'being spiritual'. It is a clear and earnest pondering or investigation into your present and actual nature. There is no journey to be made and no practices to be done—just a peace and spaciousness to be *recognized*. Right now, *as you are reading these words*, you are seeing from, through, and at the solution for which you are seeking. This is your miracle, your glory, your effluence of sacredness: *You* are the answer. Don't move from this, because *this* is what you are.

◆   As for why you're not experiencing Self—well, you can't help **but** experience it. For it is what you **are**. You are merely overlooking that 'oneness' which is immediately within and before you. Indeed, its very nearness appears to complicate one's perceiving it. But there is no real complication, of course, only an apparent one. For we simply aren't used to looking at something so close up. We only know thoughts and emotions and sensations. But **what** is it that is there **before** any of those things are there?

◆   You don't come to this understanding through any straining or inordinate efforts. All of that is completely unnecessary. Just continue to explore this issue with ease and earnestness, and you will have the answer for yourself. And it will be a living and a vital answer, one of true peace and understanding.

◆   What you are seeking **cannot** be sought. It is there and fully present **before** any attempts are made toward it. Allow your mind to be paused by this exquisite fact. Direct and poignant pointing can't help but stop your mental churning. You just don't take note of such timeless moments when they occur; nor do you see the fullness of them. And such moments take place many, many times during the day. So be alert for them, in a relaxed and easy manner. And perhaps you will come to see yourself in all of your sheerness and majesty.

◆ The mind *translates*; awareness *witnesses*.

◆ You are *spaciousness—not* the thoughts, feelings or bodily sensations that come up *within* it. If you take a careful look at this fact, you will be free.

◆ Having transcended pleasure and pain doesn't mean that one doesn't experience pleasure and pain. Such a person still enjoys pleasure and seeks quick relief from pain. But now, there is *no defined person* doing this. It is the clear and natural actions of a particular body-mind entity, whose fundamental nature is awareness itself.

◆ Be wary of an 'examination of things'. That could continue without end. A thought is a thought is a thought. End of story. There is really nothing left to examine. Just see how you are giving undue significance to your thoughts and feelings. Yes, they are vital and practical, but they aren't who and what we *are*. We know that an idea and an emotion is there, *because* there is a *knowingness* in which the thought or feeling arises. That knowingness is *awareness*.

◆ Presence doesn't dissect or scrutinize. It perfectly beholds whatever is present. Whatever comes up after the initial witnessing is the so-called mind, with its varying assessments of the original thought, concept or sentiment.

◆   This understanding occurs only when you are liberated from the idea of liberation itself. And it isn't something that happens incrementally. It is a sudden and fully sweeping away of your imagined and acrimonious self.

◆   All states of consciousness appear and disappear *within* you. You are infinitely larger and grander than the most mesmerizing spiritual experience or the most awesome galactic phenomenon. Continue to give credence to this perspective of yourself, until you see it with unquestionable clarity.

◆   Note that your thoughts and feelings *are being* perceived. It is never the other way around, with your thoughts and emotions perceiving *you*. See the *direction* from which this recognition is happening, and you will recognize your own ever-present Reality.

◆   In deep sleep, there are no objects for awareness to recognize—no thoughts, dreams or body-sense. Thus, we only know it as having been deep, restful and marvellously peaceful. Consciousness emanates from awareness the next morning, and then the body and the so-called mind are recognized. But awareness is forever there: *It Does Not Move*.

◆ Don't get caught up with names and labels. The actuality of awareness is totally beyond any debates as to whether it should be called God, Presence, *Brahman*, the Absolute or Supreme Intelligence.

◆ Seekers overly stress the notion that they must somehow 'look within'. But awareness is both within and without. It is everywhere at once, immaculate and beginningless.

◆ This understanding is not a temporary 'experiencing of God'. Rather, it is an actual knowing that God's presence and magnificence has *always* been in full evidence.

◆ Forget human and conscious evolutionary movements, and your need to join them and edify the world. Focus on what you are right here and now. Besides, how can you possibly help someone else, if you don't have a clue about your very own Reality?

◆ Attempting to get rid of the ego is a spiritual and meditative trap. Clueless teachers have fostered the myth that the ego (which is nothing but a temporary thought or feeling) can and does need to be annihilated.

◆ There is really no new 'information' when it comes to non-duality. What *is* original, though, is the perspective of the person who comes to this understanding. He or she then speaks and writes about it (if the person is inclined to do so) in his own way, which will no doubt resonate with certain seekers.

◆ Presence is what you are *at this very moment*. Allow yourself to be paused by the following: What is it, right now, that is not a thought, an emotion or a body sensation? What is it, right now, that is subtle, beginningless and most definitely present? Ponder this, keep it in your heart, and you will see for yourself that *you* have *always* been the answer.

◆ Awareness is the ever-present witness to your varying states of consciousness (waking, dreaming, dreamless sleep, etc). It is not only what *you* are, it is the Reality that pervades the whole universe. There is nothing that it isn't, nowhere where it is not.

◆ You cannot 'Be Here Now', because you *are* here now... One of the central difficulties with presence is articulating the ease with which it can be recognized.

◆ Non-duality isn't about morality, character-building or perfect equanimity. Compassion and peace are natural results of this seeing and understanding. Though one's personality stays largely the same, there is now this quiescent ground of being from which life is fully witnessed.

◆ Gathering knowledge will not lead you to Knowledge. Just see that your thoughts, emotions and sensations arise in a presence of extraordinary spaciousness that you have simply overlooked.

◆ Once presence is recognized, you don't have to do a thing to 'remain' there or to 'maintain' the seeing. The seeing and understanding fully stops you to who and what you actually are. Presence is then beautifully apparent and unmoving. Thoughts, feelings, silliness, anger and joy will still come up; but they will come up and disappear within a pristine expanse that is nothing less than Existence itself. So there is very little identification with any thoughts and emotions. They are like waves in the ocean, rising and falling, coming and going. But what is it that remains? What is it about the waves that does *not* change? It's the fact that all waves are water. It's all one sea.

◆ Say to yourself: 'I am...' But stay with the pause that has no name.

◆ There is no truth to be found in the **concept** of awareness.

◆ Truth requires no oaths, ceremonies, commitments or spiritual names.

◆ When it comes to this understanding, there is no 'spiritual union' of any kind. In fact, any idea related to your 'joining' anything automatically cancels the possibility of your discovering your true self.

◆ You think (and are told) that you need to 'become one' with your true self. But you don't. You are **already** That—which expresses itself as sereneness, spaciousness and self-shining sheerness. The **recognition** of this Freedom **is** the understanding of it. And the **understanding** of it **is** the recognition of it. One connotes the other.

◆ When you talk about blissful states, you aren't talking about awareness proper. You are speaking about experiences, nothing more and nothing less. And experiences are on the same level as thought. Both are things of the body-mind. So no matter how grand the thought or experience, you haven't discerned the **principle** in which concepts and experiences appear and then disappear.

◆ Your natural state **does** have a blissful quality to it. But that is only one of its many magnificent aspects. The others include peace and spaciousness. These are not experiences. They are the features or qualities of awareness that do not change.

◆ The thought, 'I'll never get this', is just an idea arising in what you already are: *self-shining presence*. You **are** That, right at this very moment. There is nothing that you have to attain or to work toward. Notions of having to do either of those only turn your attention away from what is right here, right now.

◆ You are already in full possession of your natural state. You just need to confirm this for yourself. Your own direct seeing and understanding leave you with absolutely no questions about the validity of your inherent reality. And when that recognition occurs, you may shout, smile, tear up, shake your head or sit in silence. Every body-personality is different.

◆ What is it that is subtly present that is not a thought, a sensation, an emotion, or an object? What is it that is none of these? *Do Not Move From This*. See it to the end which, ironically, is your beginning. It is all Oneness which, in actuality, has no beginning or end.

◆ You are not your thoughts, body, and feelings. You are the awareness that is *aware* of your thoughts, body, and feelings. Intuit the clear and simple reality of this, and you needn't concern yourself with **attempting to cease identification** with your physicality and concepts. This will happen of its own accord.

◆ You never fully come out of deep sleep (which is awareness without thoughts, images, feelings, etc). Presence remains firmly in the background during your day-to-day activities, witnessing your varying states of consciousness, as well as radiating through them. Indeed, all is awareness.

◆ True self-inquiry isn't a practice. It is, as the name implies, an inquiry that is allowed to easily unfold. Let us say you have the thought, 'I am brilliant'. What you're looking for is the quick, out-of-the-blue response, '**Who** is brilliant?' It is only when this response is natural and unexpected, that it delivers a deep pause. And if you remain with that pause, you may see that there is no 'who' present at all, but rather, a magnificent spaciousness that is both untouched and unborn. This is the Self-inquiry about which Ramana Maharshi was speaking.

◆ *See that you are only the see-ing. Nothing else.*

◆ You would not be able to perceive that you are awake and conscious, if you were not That which is *prior* to consciousness. Allow yourself to be halted by this glorious truth. Don't rush back to thoughts and thinking. Self-knowing is one of the simplest of things. There is absolutely nothing abstruse or theoretical about it. Nor is it anything that you have to strive for or achieve. Simply see what is being pointed to: an utterly peaceful and inherent *presence* that is *prior* to all thoughts and conceptualizing.

◆ Self-realization is the seeing or understanding that you are awareness itself. There is no need for you to practise, become or achieve anything. That's the glory of non-duality which is the ultimate Truth. And you, quite literally, *are* that Truth. It is supremely present at this very moment. It only appears not to be evident, because you are *overlooking* it. Back up, back up! See that there is a felt presence and sheerness that is *prior* to your changing states of consciousness. *That* is what you are! That is your essence and freedom. *Do Not Move From This*.

◆ Before any thoughts or concepts about awareness arise, awareness is *already* thoroughly present. It is a felt transparency that is, at once, subtle and profound, pristine and manifest.

◆ Deep sleep proves that **something** continues to exist when there is no ego, no mind, no bodily sensation, and no consciousness. You **are** that something **at this very moment**. You needn't look for it at night, because, in deep sleep, there is only unconditioned awareness which isn't aware of itself. Discover this for yourself. What is it, right here and now, that does not sleep?

◆ Life is Existence, Knowingness, and Peace. But all of these are manifestations from a single reality: non-conceptual awareness.

◆ Every time you attempt to 'reach' self-realization, you are—inversely—delaying it. Why? Because you are **already** awareness itself. Your seeking it entails not only an imagined seeker, but the notion that you have to make some sustained effort to 'gain' this state.

◆ Attempting to live in the 'now' is utterly foolish. **Who** is the person or individual that is trying to **achieve** this? You are timelessness itself! Why (seemingly) obfuscate your innate clarity by attempting to bring in a fictitious person to attain something that you already are? Like meditation, mindfulness, mantra-chanting, and forced silence, this seeking the 'now' is a complete waste of time and energy.

◆ Keep things simple. Begin with the bare fact that you are this sheer immediacy itself. See that there is an actual presence of awareness *before* you and *as* you. It is ripe with peace, love, and fullness. Keep coming back to this, in an easy and natural manner, until it is a rich and living reality.

◆ Even happiness is only an experience. Thus, it is limited in duration and in no way compares to the peace of presence itself.

◆ To *what* does a thought appear? It obviously is not your body, because your body is physical matter. And it can't be your mind, because your mind is nothing but the occurrence of a thought! So to *what* does a thought appear? Allow the power and significance of this question to bring you to a full stop. You really don't have to do a thing. Just see that there is **something** to which a thought must appear. It can't be another thought, because one thought can't know another one. So to what are your present thoughts appearing?

◆ Self-knowing: *This-ness* without end.

◆ Stop a moment and *feel* the spaciousness from which your previous thought arose.

◆   If you could see the foolishness of your seeking, you would be struck speechless with disbelief. You are floating in the clearest, purist, most magical of springs, and yet, you search for water. Pause a moment and recognize not only the presence of this sheer, aqueous plenitude, but that you are the spring itself.

◆   There really is no spiritual ignorance—just a misunderstanding as to what you truly are.

◆   *What* is present? Not *who*. Again, take note of *what* is present, not *who*.

◆   Non-duality is not about feelings, serenity, healing, ascension, 'regressive therapies', or even esoteric philosophies. If you're seeking more experiences and conceptual theories, then by all means indulge. Have them. However, they are not paths to truth, because there aren't any. The undertaking of any path or practice is— seemingly, at least—a move *away* from this shimmering substratum.

◆ The 'me', for the most part, is the *imagined continuity* thought. Instead of simply having a memory of previous ideas and emotions, you give them an aliveness, a reach and—most important—a relationship. While thoughts are certainly central to our living and communicating with one another, *thoughts do not define us*. What is the stillness from which all thoughts arise? Discover that glorious Quintessence for yourself.

◆ This understanding cannot be found in theories or concepts—not even *advaitic* ones! It is, *in toto*, the unconditioned **spaciousness** that is *prior* to any thought or experience.

◆ *Q: And, in my mind, immediately pops up, 'How is it done'?*

Rodney: The seeing or the understanding *is* the 'doing'. There is no 'how' other than that. Indeed, the 'how' is just another thought raised by the mind. But when no thought is present, what *is* present?... See that there is an undeniable pause there. At first glance, the pause seems quite ordinary. But if you bring your full attention to it, freshly and without stress, you may find that that pause isn't ordinary at all. But rather, it is eternal, omnipresent and ever-peaceful. Again, don't make it a chore or an effort. Just keep coming back to those potent moments as they naturally occur throughout the day and evening.

Then you will see that you never ever move from your self-shining Essence. And what could be more precious than that?

◆   All of your notions about bliss, *moksha*, liberation, enlightenment and transformation, are keeping you from cognitizing your natural and ever-present state. By focusing on the aforementioned, you are centring on myths and inaccuracies, rather than on what is right here, right now.

◆   Don't give presence any religious or spiritual baggage. It can neither be categorized nor sanctified. Yet, it is Sanctification itself. And you can come to this understanding just as easily on the toilet as you can at an *ashram* or spiritual commune. Indeed, I would say that the likelihood is far greater with the former than with the latter.

◆   This is key: The 'I' or imagined person cannot get this. Self-knowing only happens in the **absence** of thoughts and concepts. That is why the pause is so vital when it comes to this understanding.

◆ Thoughts and ideas can only **point** to Reality, not **describe** it. Don't think for a moment that you can get even a modicum of an approximation of what presence is by a term, expression or description. And this fact, in itself, points to the eternal and numinous qualities of awareness, all of which are readily before you and within you at this very moment.

◆ Apropos meditation: You can't get **here**, from **there**. You are absolutely always **here**. The 'there' is a fiction, a projection, an appearance that comes and goes. Your very nature is **here-ness**, and yet you are missing it— not because it's abstract or abstruse, but because your scrutiny is given to concepts and sensations.

◆ You can't stop the mind. The mind is a naturally occurring process. And **who**, precisely, is there to stop it? The 'I' and 'me' **are** the mind! They are just thoughts coming up. And these thoughts are coming up in awareness, not in some defined and individual 'you'. The only 'you' there **is** awareness. And you are That.

◆ Thoughts are only a problem, when you attempt to stop, slow or monitor them.

◆ The end of misunderstanding is the end of a defined and individual you.

◆ U.G. Krishnamurti wisely pointed out that, unlike saints, 'Sages don't depend on any authority; what they say *is* the authority.' This is because they are speaking from the source of their beingness. And there is no higher authority than that.

◆ Meditation, mantras, mindfulness, and even *kundalini*-yoga, are all within the mental realm. Awareness is totally beyond that—so much so, in fact, that you can't use any of those activities or approaches as a steppingstone to presence.

◆ Your natural state is already before you and within you. But you keep returning to the level of the mind when you attempt to meditate, watch your thoughts, or repeat a mantra. Ironically, it is the moment *after* doing any one of these things that you are back to your ever-spacious and pristine naturalness.

◆ When you *attempt* 'to be present', you—as a thought, an imagined entity—are trying to *align* yourself with presence. But how can a thought, which is a mere appearance, align itself with awareness, which is an actuality? Instead of attempting 'to be present', wouldn't it make far more sense to bring your attention to the fact that you *are* presence *itself*?

◆ The mind can raise the question of who and what you are, but it can't answer it.

◆ Insights aren't synonymous with understanding. Self-realization isn't a conceptual issue, nor is it arrived at by intellectual sparring and conclusions. Rather, it is a fundamental understanding that all is presence. And that understanding is immensely alive and penetrating—*It is not up for debate*.

◆ In reality, there are only perceptions. There are no distinct and separate objects in existence. All is awareness, however many variations, dimensions and manifestations awareness may take.

◆ Awareness is *always* choiceless. So there is absolutely no need for you to 'cultivate' or 'practise' choicelessness. Besides, *who* would be doing the practising? If you say that *you* would, that assumed person is not real. It only comes up occasionally (or often) as an 'I' or a 'me' or a 'mine'. It cannot help you to see, cultivate or practise anything. It is a thought, a response, a piece of information that may be either correct or incorrect. Presence is *already* there, of course. It is the spaciousness *within which* those concepts and responses are occurring. Again, *you are the spaciousness*, not the appearances within it. See the beauty, immediacy and simplicity of this stunning actuality.

◆　　Self-realization isn't the 'extinction of the mind'. Thoughts continue to come up, thank God. It's just that, now, you understand that you are the spaciousness *from which* all thoughts arise, and that the temporary appearance of feelings and ideas is the mind proper. When they aren't there, neither is the mind.

◆　You say that you want 'peace of mind'. But you can never have that. The thoughts, sensations and feelings of the so-called mind are, by turns, calming, exciting, ludicrous, resentful, sexual, sacred, acrimonious, and loving. This is a natural part of your functioning. This is what the mind *is*: the *arisings* of all of those previously mentioned things. So when you meditate in an attempt to either stop your mind, or to watch it long enough to see where it appears to be stopped, you will inevitably fail. But you most certainly *can* have peace. Just take note that *you are actually not your thoughts*. You are that eternally spacious and cognizant peace that *knows* that an idea or a feeling is present. And with the seeing of this, the importance of any arising concept or sentiment is quickly given its proper due.

◆ You can only know something, **because** you **already** transcend it. You are that presence that knows or registers a thought or emotion. And because you **are** transcendence itself, there is nothing that you have to 'reach' or work toward. This understanding is not evolutionary at all. The great sages, from Shankara and Sri Atmananda Menon to Nisargadatta Maharaj and Sailor Bob Adamson, all say that **you absolutely are already That**. There is nothing you need to do except **see** or **understand** what is already before you. The loveliness of this fact points to your very own radiance. Pause a moment and see what is forever shining.

◆ Your natural state appears not to be there because, in large part, your attention is simply (and temporarily) centring on the next thought, sound, or sensation. Awareness is never being blocked or inhibited at all.

◆ How could there be a path or process to what you already **are**?

◆ Self-knowledge isn't 'cultivated'. Additionally, there is no 'going back into it' or 'deepening of it' at all. Any attempt to do either is giving credence to a referential 'I' that, essentially, does not exist. It is a construct, a practicality that we employ so as to enable us to communicate with one another and to go about our lives. Therefore, this 'I' needn't be shunned nor revered. It is what it is. And you are what you are: radiant spaciousness without beginning or end.

◆   When I say that presence is 'within and before you', I mean it *literally*: *This Moment Is It*. Awareness isn't something that is going to magically appear after x number of months or years of meditation, or after x number of sessions of sitting. It brims before you *at this very second*.

◆   Read the next sentence slowly:

Presence - lies - between - the - spaces - of - the - words - in - the - sentence - that - you - are - reading - right - now.

You, no doubt, felt something deep, unmoving and indescribable as you carefully perused the above.

◆   We go through life largely overlooking these natural and very potent pauses, multitudes of them throughout the day, actually. And we do this mainly out of habit. So I try to bring the reader's or seeker's attention back to this pristine and ever-present spaciousness which, in effect, is being ignored. But, once it is recognized or understood, it will indeed appear to be thoroughly within and before you. There will then be no doubt that awareness is absolutely everything everywhere. Truly, no grandness—however cosmic, erudite, or spiritual— can ever excel your essence. For *you are that One-without-any-second at this very moment*.

◆ Not to belabour the obvious, but you can't 'meditate' your way to enlightenment. From the very beginning, meditation is based on the utterly false premises that [1] there is an individual meditator, and [2] that there is something to attain. The recognition of your natural state is all about *seeing* and *understanding* what is *presently* within and before you.

◆ Though your natural state is subtle, it is self-luminous and ever before you. Any method or practice '*toward*' it is an immediate move '*away*' from it (in so much as one *can* move from it). Even any attempted forms of surrender won't work, because there is 'someone' trying to do the deed. True surrender is effortless. It is a sudden seeing or understanding that presence is a felt and living reality. Take a moment to discover it for yourself. Trust me when I say this: Absolutely nothing could be simpler.

◆ Meditation can certainly help you to relax. But the results are usually short-lived. However, if you enjoy meditation, then by all means continue to do it. Just know that it isn't a steppingstone to knowing your natural state. That can only be recognized when meditation ceases.

◆ When you attempt to be 'mindful' of your thoughts or breathing, you are piling this assumed person onto an already perfect, on-going action. Simply see that there is a presence of awareness, within you and before you, that **automatically** witnesses all notions and objects. And it takes no time nor any period of sitting to see this.

◆ It is your **attention** that you bring to presence, not some distinct, individual person who is somehow separated from the world and from presence.

◆ A wave is **always** water: We are **always** awareness. When a belief of separation is focused upon, it tends to be strengthened. And that's certainly true when it comes to the assumption that, among other things, Reality is something that has to be garnered or attained. False teachers (and they are profuse) ply their piffle to disparate and non-discerning seekers who are filled with all of these romantic and stereotypic notions of what this understanding truly is. The teachers will tell you, in spectacular terms, that 'Enlightenment' (*their* word, not mine) can be attained—through time even!—by meditation, sitting, silence, mindfulness, yoga, mantras and/or servitude to them. You may even have some short-term bliss. But that will only be an **experience**. It won't be your **natural** state.

◆ There is nothing mystical or otherworldly about awareness. It is pure, perfect, vivid, and beginningless. It is totally beyond the staggering contents of the innumerable galaxies and any hypothesized multiverses. It's even beyond spirituality. Yet, amazingly, it is the most ordinary of things.

◆ **To know thyself is to know that your belief in a separate self is utterly without merit.** You are a bright and beautiful wave on the translucent ocean of presence. There is absolutely no other wave like you in this sheer and eternal sea. Not one. Yet, you and the ocean are nothing but awareness. Never, for a second, have you **not** been this radiant, blue presence. Your depth and loveliness know no bounds. Truly, no description can approach you.

◆ Take advantage of any times when you are naturally calm and quiet. It could be when you are at an art museum, on a natural trail, walking through freshly-fallen snow, or strolling along a beach. Allow for the timeless recognition of your luminous Self *by* your Self. See that *you* are the seeing, the knowing, and the stillness.

◆ I love that word 'faith'. Alas, it has been misused by religions and religionists. To a certain extent, faith is a belief. But even more, it is an unexplainable and inner **knowing** that what is being pointed to is nothing but the bare and non-conceptual Truth.

◆ You *are* the Absolute. That is key. Right at this moment, you *are* That. Those are the potent fundamentals that point to your radiant and ceaseless reality.

◆ One of the reasons that you are struggling with non-duality is that you are thinking of it in terms of an occurrence or an event. Or even as a feeling or an experience. But it is completely *beyond* the pinnacle emotions of joy and happiness. It's even beyond love. So any attempts to utilize or 'align with' specific sentiments or conditions will be of no help to you.

◆ Deep sleep is far superior to any blissful or ecstatic experience. For deep sleep is deep rest. And it is completely natural. During deep sleep, awareness is still present. But there is nothing to witness—no thoughts, no dreams, and no bodily perceptions or sensations. We literally die a sweet death every night. We even crave it, because it is the only thing that gives us such peace and rest. But you can *know* that which never sleeps or dies *at this very moment*. Discover it for yourself.

◆ *Every object is a pointer to the Absolute*—even our egos.

◆ You are a living embodiment of Truth itself. You are simply overlooking your natural and ever-present state. But that's not your fault, entirely. You have been taught by family, mentors, teachers and spiritual counsellors to see yourself not only as an individual, but as an individual with an x-kind of car, y-kind of job and z-kind of suburban life, all of which go to only increase your sense of individualism. But the good news is that you are awareness proper. All you need to do is see this for yourself.

◆ Clarity and contentment *are* non-duality. This great teaching is nothing less than a felt reality from which you are never absent. It only *appears* that it is something for which you have to search or that you have to attain. But nothing could be further from the Truth—which, ironically, is the very same thing that could be said about yourself at this very moment.

◆ Liberation isn't the end of bondage. It is the seeing or understanding that you have *always* been Freedom itself—bare, utter and complete.

◆ The Absolute can never be described or communicated to anybody. All one can do is *point*.

◆ You can't annihilate the ego (which is just an appearance anyway) or attain some egoless state. Those are spiritual fictions. *Simply direct your attention to your ever-present presence of awareness* until it is clear and undeniable. Then thoughts and feelings are naturally balanced.

◆ Awareness witnesses *through* consciousness. Thus, consciousness is clearly not the ultimate 'I'. Consciousness is a state or movement *within* awareness. It is closely linked to the body, and its attributes include awakeness, dreaming, drowsiness, and sleeping. Awareness is spaciousness, but it is not a void. It is a very real and cognitizing presence that can't begin to be put into words.

◆ There is no 'one' to rest as or in awareness. Any thinking in that direction, however limited, leads you nowhere. For *Truth can only be seen by Truth*. And when this seeing occurs, it is quick, unquestionable, and completely free of any 'I' or 'you'.

◆ Perception proves the existence of awareness, and *not* the existence of the perceived objects themselves.

◆ Wisdom is *self*-knowledge. It is not objective or conceptual knowledge.

◆ When a thought is present, you know it. When a thought is not present, what is it that knows that the thought is *not* there?

◆ All that arises—from your very next thought to the most spectacular nebulosity—emanates from this pristine, formless presence that we call awareness. You may also call it God, *Brahman*, Clear Light, the Holy Spirit, or Supreme Intelligence. The name is utterly unimportant.

◆ *What is paramount is to see that there is no separation between Beingness and the person you take yourself to be*. Why? Because the person is a fiction, a recurring assemblage of, among other things, senses, memory, and personality traits, with no enduring continuity.

◆ True renunciation is not depriving yourself of the earth's splendours or living in abject poverty. It is the clear recognition that you are truth itself.

◆ Self-realization is a matter of being *what* you are—not *who* you are

◆ Personalities tend not to change after self-realization. Thoughts, emotions and feelings still come up. But they are seen for what they are: *mere appearances in awareness*. Identification with thoughts and sentiments may continue for a while, until your understanding is clear. This is simply an adjustment period. Soon you'll see that there is less and less identification with whatever arises, with absolutely no effort on your part.

◆ You don't need a mantra, a spiritual name, a month-long retreat, or an expensive (or cheap) flight to India, for this understanding to occur. Further, Truth isn't patiently waiting somewhere for you to discover it. It is neither here, nor there—yet, it's lustrous, in plain view, and everywhere.

◆ Why *move* from *this*? You say you must practise mindfulness, repeat your mantra, raise your *kundalini*, or centre on your chakras. My only question is, 'Why *move* from *this*?'

◆ When you are told to pause a thought, you aren't being instructed to stop your thinking. (Well, at least not by credible teachers.) Just notice that, before the next thought appears, there is a bare spaciousness directly before or within you. Now relax into it. It is that simple.

◆ Every single time you meditate, you are doing the very *opposite* of what will help you to discover who and what you are.

◆ One of the glorious things about awareness is that it is something upon which you are *already* gazing. All you need to do is to perceive its immediacy and fullness, or to see that there is not one individual person in existence.

◆ By giving emphasis to your thinking, you give sustenance to the idea that, somehow, you *are* your lofty thoughts and concepts. But the mind cannot exist by itself. Thus, there must be some presence even greater than the mind. See that there is something *in which* your thoughts are arising. It is sheer, timeless, and ever-peaceful. It is your natural state.

◆ You have to see the absurdity of your own seeking.

◆ There is no subject-object relationship with awareness: Awareness is all there is. Yes, thoughts, emotions and sensations appear, but they are simply manifestations *within* presence-awareness itself. And you *are* That: the unchanging Subject-without-a-second.

◆ When you realize that there is nothing you can do about your normal thinking, then there is an automatic de-energizing of all thoughts.

◆ You **are** awareness. Therefore, there is no person to awaken. All of your sitting, chanting and meditating to **get** enlightened are such a ludicrous waste of time, money and energy. You can come to this understanding by simply (and reflectively) eating a piece of pizza.

◆ You don't have to 'make room' for presence—for presence is all there is. And **who** would be 'making room' for it anyway? All 'you' would be doing is simply getting in the way!

◆ The only way to transcend the ego is to understand that it can't possibly be who and what you are. How could you conceivably be something that comes and goes—that is 'good' one moment and 'bad' the other? Anything that changes is, unequivocally, not your abiding essence. Throughout the day, take note of the fact that **there is something that doesn't move**, despite the plethora of thoughts, feelings and sensations. What is that 'something'?

◆ If you're looking for unending happiness, you're barking up the wrong tree. Happiness is a shifting condition. On the other hand, deep peace—which is your natural state—never alters in the least.

◆   Non-duality points to an *immediate* recognition that can always be had. It is merely a matter of seeing or understanding what is *abundantly* present. Nothing has to be formalized or ritualized. And you don't require the support of any community to have it happen (though if a community of serious and well-meaning seekers is naturally in place, terrific!).

◆   The Self, like the 'Tenth Man', does not have to be created or searched for. You *are* the tenth person! No one was ever lost. Just see what it is that has never been absent. It's right there within you at this very moment. Time is not a factor with self-knowing. Anyone who tells you that you need x number of weeks/months/years/decades for this seeing to occur, has absolutely no idea what he or she is talking about. None!

◆   If you are attempting to 'unite' with presence, that imagined 'I' will continually keep you from seeing that presence is what you *already* are.

◆   All thinking is a movement **away** from your natural state. That's not to say that thoughts are evil and should be squashed at all cost. Thinking allows us to function in society in a safe and prudent manner. It's just that, when thoughts and emotions arise, your attention is momentarily on them. Bring your focus back to the presence of peace and expansiveness **between** your thoughts and responses. And this seeing and understanding happens immediately, fully, and with absolutely no fanfare. Yet, it is totally beyond anything that you could ever imagine.

◆   You are awareness **already**. It doesn't get any simpler than that.

◆   Who is it that is doubting that self-knowledge can't be had? If you examine the issue carefully, you will see (and with considerable ease) that the doubt is just an arising thought. Thus, your uncertainty can't be you, because you can't be something that comes and goes. So what remains? Ever-present awareness, which has merely been ignored.

◆   Conditioning isn't a constant. It is a thought, feeling, or action, arising in the spaciousness that you presently are. Freedom is your nature, your inherent condition. You're giving **emphasis** to the thoughts and emotions, because you think or imagine that they are the only things that are there. But that simply isn't the case.

◆ Your mind can never find awareness. Can a shadow reach the sun?

◆ See how hypothetical you are making everything: How needless questions arise out of your intellectualizing (not to mention mythologizing!) your search for self-knowledge. When this is seen, there is a very natural pause that points to presence itself.

◆ In order to know that your thoughts and sentiments are *temporarily* there, there must be a fundamental knower that is *always* there. This knower isn't your body or your mind or your consciousness. It is pure awareness. And yes, you *are* this Knower. Allow yourself to see the immense beauty and fullness of this. You will marvel at how you could have missed it for so long.

◆ Awareness is independent of your thoughts, concepts, and spiritual lineage. It's there, whether you believe in it or not. It's all a matter of seeing and understanding presence *As It Is*. Anything less than that is experiential, fleeting, and conceptual. You are what you are at this very second. But you take yourself to be your job, body, personality, gender, nationality, or bank account. And none of that is true.

◆ You are looking *away* from what you are seeking. You're looking at everything *but* It.

◆ The answer to all of your spiritual and philosophical questions is directly within and before you. All that is needed is for you to recognize how clearly your own Clarity is *already* present. No spiritual or geographical journeys are required for that. Radiance is what you are *at this very moment*. So go ahead, have a quick and timeless look at your ever-present nature. It is lustrous and unfeigned, and it will never desert you.

◆ You are certainly present, for you are reading these words at this very moment. But what *is* it that is present? Take a calm and quiet moment to ponder what, precisely, is being overlooked. And with the answer, you go from being merely present to Presence itself.

◆ There is a hushness to presence, as well as a hallowed palpability. It is there, and it isn't. Once you see that it is 'this', you also see how it is 'that'. Then you understand how it is neither. Turn in any direction and it is there. And so are You.

◆ Non-duality requires neither decades of devotion nor a disciplining of the mind. *Awareness is your very nature*. You are more It than you are your body and your breathing. See what it is that you keep coming back to throughout the day and evening—those precious periods *between* every transient thought, sentiment, and belief.

◆ There is a presence of awareness directly within and before you, as you are reading these words. It never moves from being *right here, right now*.

◆ The mind can help you enormously with your *seeking*. It will take you from one experience and concept to another, and it will do this until the end of your days. It cannot, however, recognize and understand your abiding nature, for the mind comes and goes *within* that nature, in that eternal peace and spaciousness that just happens to be your ever-present state.

◆ Right now, what you are is *prior* to any doubts, questions and imaginings you might have about non-duality.

◆ You say, 'From now on, I'm not going to care about what the mind does.' But who is the perceived individual that is going to be doing that? Notice that *a position is being taken here*, and that that can only happen when there is a doer, a 'someone' who is going to set things right. The mind is going to do what it is going to do. Thoughts and emotions are going to continue to rise. They aren't you. They can't *possibly* be you! You are That which *recognizes* them. Bring your attention back to your timeless essence and see the bare, beautiful truth of who and what you are.

◆ Just because some people assert that they have no more questions, doesn't mean that they have come to a true understanding of who and what they are. This applies to seeker and teacher alike. *There has to be a complete seeing of how life is apparently appearing and dividing itself into subjects and objects, forms and no-forms*.

◆ Don't turn self-knowing into a process. If you do, it will certainly be a never-ending one. Why? Because then your focus and attention is on the methodology, rather than on what is *already* fully and radiantly present. No process can 'take' you to awareness: You *are* awareness! Thus, the use of any method to 'reach' your natural state is simply idiotic.

◆ Even an ongoing 'acceptance of all things' can be the 'me' in muffled operation. *There are no positions to be taken by any apparent 'I' when it comes to self-knowing*.

◆ The body, mind, personality and consciousness, are all appearances *in* presence. You aren't any of those arisings. You are That which knows that they are momentarily there. Bring your attention to the spaciousness *around* the thought or emotion.

◆ *You are the sumptuous and unaltering background to your apparent and ever-changing life*. Your very own peaceable kingdom resides immediately within you. And that stillness is without end. For the space inside of a jar is the same space outside of the jar. The jar is largely inconsequential. The space is not.

◆ You are awareness itself. You can't possibly be anything but That.

◆ Just to be clear: Awareness has 'happened' already! You are that *right at this very moment*. Indeed, it is so in evidence, that you are *overlooking* it. And this 'bypassing' of presence is going on in all spiritual sectors, with seekers the world over.

◆ That timeless and marvellously concise, non-dual gem, '*You are That*', points us to an immediacy to which we have never given our attention. And when you do come to your clear seeing, you will certainly see that there never was a *who*, and always a *what*: awareness itself.

◆ Presence is not a void. Indeed, it is the only real thing that there is.

◆ You have to see yourself by yourself. No teacher can give it to you or structure some method or process with which this understanding will occur. Your own immediate and unending spaciousness is the answer.

◆ Stop *trying* to be free, and simply see that you are Freedom itself. How can awareness, which you already *are*, be in any way acquired or contained? More foolish still is to think that presence can somehow be 'entered' or 'maintained'!

◆ Who is dissolving what? There are too many characters in this play. The stage is all there is. See the beauty, silence and unchanging vastness of it. Nothing has to be rehearsed, fine-tuned or performed. You are what you are *at this very moment*. You always *have* been and you always *will* be awareness itself.

◆ The 'ego' can't be dissolved. So forget about that approach altogether. For you are attempting to stop something that naturally occurs and then disappears. It's a practicality that helps you to function in life. Simply bring your attention to the spaciousness within which the 'I' sense comes and goes, and you will be on the right track.

◆ There is nothing but presence, and no one to know it... Individuality is assumed, but not actual.

◆ Simply see what it is that has never been absent.

◆ **Who** is standing apart from awareness? **You** certainly are not. All that's happening is that there is a thought saying that you and presence are somehow separate.

◆ Awareness can't be experienced. It isn't an object or something new that comes into being. It can only be known or understood to unequivocally exist. Allow these words to resonate within you throughout the day, if you are so inclined. To be effective, such contemplations have to be absolutely natural and unforced.

◆ You can't get any closer to what you are right at this moment. Even when your understanding occurs, there will be no attainment of anything. You will simply perceive that awareness has **always** been **abundantly** present, and that you were/are That. There is just a clear and beautiful seeing of all this.

◆ Your natural state is your natural state. It never moves from being absolutely there.

◆   All pointers are conceptual. Yet, the best ones aim *away* from themselves, to awareness itself. You can't remain with ideas and concepts, and expect to come to this understanding. The same applies with repeating mantras and engaging in practices, for with those activities, too, you are existing on a dualistic and conceptual level.

◆   You don't have to do a single thing, except recognize what is already present.

◆   You're searching for air when air is all around you. Just breathe in, i.e. recognize that there is a quiet presence of peace and spaciousness directly within and before you. You never move from being this bare 'what-ness' and plenitude. So try taking note of how things are constantly changing throughout your daily life, and you just may discern That which *isn't* changing in the least.

◆   This understanding has nothing to do with anything that is visionary, ecstatic, mystical, or heavenly. Neither are such occurrences prerequisites for self-knowledge.

◆   To say that one liberates oneself is still too much. It is simply a seeing or recognition that 'liberation' is your very nature. For awareness is totally without limits or qualities, and you never move from being precisely That.

◆ **Q**: *How do I place my attention on awareness?*

Rodney: By recognizing that it is present. It seems easier to give your attention to a piece of beautiful music or writing than to awareness because, in those examples, you are naturally and habitually utilizing your hearing and seeing. You don't even think about it. Because awareness is not an object, you have to bring your attention to it in a completely different manner. One of the ways of doing that is with the following question: ***What is it that is fully present that you need no senses to see?***

Q: *Ah, yes... I can feel the stillness within that question.*

Rodney: And that peripheral stillness is pointing to your ultimate stillness. They are actually one and the same. Just take a close and easy look at the pause itself, keeping in mind that ***this is not a mental action at all***. In fact, no thought or action will help you at this point. ***It is staying with the pause that's paramount***. And if done correctly, you will discern that this moment of quietude is actually the presence of awareness of which all the great sages and teachers have spoken. There may appear to be a 'shifting' to a kind of immensity or depth. But really, it is more of a discovery, a recognition—indeed, a coming home.

◆   The moment you give credence to the notion that awakening is progressive or just ahead of you someplace, you are bound for disappointment.

◆ There is no one there to 'accept' or 'receive' awareness. Those are false actions regarding a false self. Awareness is what you *are*, and not something that you can 'merge' with.

◆   *Q: Hi, Rodney. I've been reading your books, as well as John Wheeler's 'Awakening to the Natural State'. What I find so surprising and refreshing is the way you both keep returning to the simplicity of observing what's really happening, not giving in to the mind's attempts to 'figure it out', and attending to presence.*

Rodney: Right. The mind is in no position to either comprehend awareness or witness it. Indeed, it arises wholly *within* awareness.

Q: The simplicity of your directions seems to be working. I'm going to attempt to describe what is being seen here, and I wonder if you could please comment.

Rodney: Sure.

Q: First, it is so simple, that it is nearly impossible to describe. Mostly, there is a strong sense of presence, which is clearly awareness. It is silent, with nothing at all to say. It is entirely at peace with itself.

Rodney: Very good—and that's beautifully articulated, by the way.

Q: *There is no movement, no desire to move, no sense of anything desired or required for completeness. It is also quite obvious that this present awareness, this 'no thing', is at the centre of everything, is what I might want to call 'me' except for the hilarious fact that 'I' don't really exist.*

Rodney: Again, all of that is on the mark.

Q: *Of course, I must at the same time say that 'I am'. But it really seems that the 'I' is utterly unimportant.*

Rodney: It is, to a substantial degree. But our temporary sense of self allows us to function in life. Whether it's writing, speaking, paying our bills, or arranging a lunch get-together, our provisional 'self ' functions as the doer. But the doer is just a thought, and a thought isn't conscious. It only **appears** to be sentient, because presence is shining through it.

Q: *Exactly. And it seems better to just call it presence or present awareness and be done with it. Or even better, why call it anything? It just **is**. It always **is**, and it is always* *the same utterly quiet, peaceful sense of being. Why the need to name it?*

Rodney: We name it in order to speak about it or to point to it. We also name it, because we want others to understand what we are talking about when we talk about awareness proper. For we aren't speaking about the tree in the yard or even everyday consciousness, of course. We are pointing to something that is **ceaseless**, and which is also our natural and luminous state.

Q: I do find that mind comes in and distracts attention from presence now and then.

Rodney: That's going to happen. Your body is going to continue to react to stimuli from your surroundings, and thoughts are going to appear as a result of those reactions. Presence really doesn't disappear; rather, your attention momentarily goes to other things. But you never move from being absolute awareness. And it never moves from being absolutely present. So the question becomes: What is it right now that is always the same, even if you were in deep sleep? **What is it that would still be present, even if you weren't conscious that it was present?**

◆   Take a careful look at your day-to-day life. What is it that never changes? There is a subtle presence of utter serenity and spaciousness that is yours for the seeing. *It has never not been present. It has simply been bypassed*. Come to it once, and it is yours. You don't have to reacquaint yourself with it again and again in order to 'deepen' it, though many teachers will have you believe that.

◆   When there is the awareness of a thought, there is no 'you' in addition to that awareness.

◆   Doubts, questions and reservations are just thoughts! They have no power beyond themselves. Thoughts arise *in* awareness. So *give your attention to the pauses after the thoughts, and see what is being ignored*.

◆   Something never moves from being what it is. What is that 'something'?

◆   *Q: So all of this seems very natural—experiencing is happening, thoughts arise, and sensations come and go, as do perceptions. What's really amusing is to watch the coming up of the thought, 'I'm getting closer to understanding this', because awareness is no closer or any more distant than it has ever been!*

Rodney: Precisely! Self-inquiry *isn't* progressive. You just *can't* make any step-by-step approaches to Reality, despite what 99% of the world's spiritual teachers say. Awareness never varies from being absolutely present. Your ego or sense-of-self can't 'move' towards awareness, because they are temporary appearances *in* it. Upon recognizing or understanding that, you immediately begin to see that your life is *being* lived, and always *has* been lived, from this state of unchanging Beingness. Feelings and emotions continue to arise, but they no longer *define* you.

◆ As you near this understanding, you will probably find yourself having less and less questions. This is because the idea of any defined 'someone' seeking 'such-and-such' will be far less potent. There will just be this gut feeling that you are both less and more (immensely more!) than you've imagined yourself to be.

◆ You are limitless, featureless, cognitizing awareness. You are prior to any concept, belief, teaching, and practice. See the utter foolishness of trying to 'reach' presence by pilgrimages and methodologies.

◆   You are beyond the mind at this very moment! So any attempt to 'go' there would be counter-productive and nonsensical. See that there has **always** been a stillness and clarity that were immediately present. Just an easy and subtle recognition is all that's needed.

◆   Can you say that you are not present, as you read these words? No, you **are** present. Now look even more attentively, and you will see that what is actually the case is that there is **only** an ever-abiding presence of awareness, and that you **are** that awareness.

◆   Your natural and glorious state isn't the production of thought. You can't think or imagine your way into it. But when there is a natural pause in thinking or imagining, presence is there for the seeing. **Awareness is never not there**, of course. It only **appears** to be absent, because your attention is on the thoughts and the imagining, rather than on what they are appearing **within**.

◆   Nothing is changed, destroyed or improved upon with this understanding. You are simply seeing something that has **always** been in existence. Thus, you can't 'practise' your way to freedom. For you are Freedom itself. Come back to this point again and again, if necessary. **You are awareness itself**. You absolutely never move from That.

◆   Awakening—or whatever term you prefer to use—is simply a matter of seeing something that has *always* been present. Any practice or goal-oriented action toward it is a move *away* from it. Time isn't a factor in this. It just isn't. Any talk of time is a way for the ego—that temporary sense of individuality—to sneak into the mix of things. And neither it nor any periods of duration can help you to witness your abiding clarity.

◆   Awareness never disappears, even when your attention is on a thought or emotion. So there is nothing to wait for and nothing to get. And there is certainly nothing to curse yourself about. For you are what you are at this very moment. Awakening is comparable to suddenly seeing the Mona Lisa in one of those 3D pictures of squiggly lines and circles. You were told that the face was always present. But now you are seeing it for yourself. And nothing could be more beautiful.

◆   The mind and body aren't the issue. You are simply *bypassing* presence, which is there 24/7. Your natural state is serene unboundedness. You never deviate from being precisely that.

◆ The ego is just a thought or feeling. Don't give it any kind of special significance. It is merely an appearance *in* presence. It comes, and it goes. *You* don't. You are what never changes. Stay with the truth and beauty of this fact: *You are That which never changes*.

◆ I am not attempting to direct you to some higher spiritual level. What I'm pointing to is something that is subtle, immediate, and without beginning or end. If you look attentively within yourself, you can see that there is indeed something there, that is all of those things.

◆ You are imposing a fictitious self upon your body and mind. And when you are told that that is not the way to end suffering, you promptly attempt to control or destroy this recurring sense of individuality by meditation, mindfulness, and mantras. In fact, the more the ego appears to be a problem, the harder you meditate. But the ego isn't the least bothered by all of that, because it is a naturally occurring appearance in the body-mind. (Also, it's not a living thing.) It's the meditation, mindfulness and mantras, that are the odd entities out!

◆ What is existing, but is not changing in the least?

◆ Most spiritual seekers are after experiences. They want to be able to enter and re-enter some unusual and ecstatic state, so that they are able to say, 'I did this!', or, 'I attained this!' But **who** is doing the coming and going? That is the question that they should be asking themselves. Who, precisely, is doing the coming and going? Because, if there is a 'who' and a coming-and-going, it isn't your natural state.

◆ You are what **knows** that an appearance is there. You are that **Knowingness**. And this Knowingness is the essence of all existence. **So you already are what you are seeking**. And that is the so-called understanding!

◆ Even **before** you can frame your question, awareness is **already** fully present. Further, you **are** that awareness. You never move from being precisely That—a peace, a hushness and an evenness that is always immediately before and within you. Truly, there is never a time when it is missing.

◆ **You can't reach what you already are**. Remain with the **what-ness**, and you'll recognize what has always been in perfect, unchanging abundance.

◆ **Q**: *In your recent blog entry, I was particularly moved by your, 'Even to say "Just be" is a directive towards some fruitless action'.*

Rodney: Yes, this subtly implies that there is 'someone' who can move closer to some imagined state. But Beingness is what we **are**. Therefore, it cannot be grasped or acquired by 'someone'.

Q: *And it can never be lost either, I gather.*

Rodney: Exactly. Nothing is really missing except your recognition of something that is categorically present **all the time**. And this fact tends to cause a double reaction in seekers: First, there is a kind of subtle (or deep) relaxation, because the person is told (by a credible source) that meditating, mantras, mindfulness, and New-Age maxims to 'Just be', aren't going to help you. Indeed, they will simply cloud the issue. And second, there is a sudden curiosity about what it is, precisely, that has **always** been in place.

Q: *For some years, back in the 70's and early 80's, I was involved with a group that laid extraordinary significance on the experience gained in meditation, but never questioned* **who** *was having the experience. You go and sit on your special cushion, in your special room where your special incense is burning and your special piece of music is playing: It's all 'mind stuff'! It's all experiencing.*

Rodney: It's all experiencing and 'mind stuff'. And no thought, action or intellectual activity is in direct relation to awareness, which is totally **beyond** all physical and mental activities. And yet, presence is nothing more than your ordinary, everyday awareness, which is what you are right now. That's one of the keys to the **non**-puzzle: That presence is simply the **what-ness** or **knowing-ness** that is existing **within** and **as** you **at this very moment**. But people take themselves to be their bodies, minds, consciousness, and even personalities. So when most of these individuals become interested in spirituality, they will use their physicality, minds and levels of consciousness to 'acquire' something that they supposedly don't currently possess. And self-realization just doesn't happen that way.

Q: That's one of the reasons I like your blog. You hone in on the non-relationship between practices and awareness.

Rodney: And the same applies to experiences, of course. Having grander experiences doesn't equate to a deeper or more solid understanding of your essential nature. Indeed, there is no understanding at all in such cases. It's just the experiencing of experiences!

◆ Spiritual practices are all on the level of the mind and on 'doing' things. But awareness can't be journeyed to. It can only be **recognized** and **understood**.

◆   There is no 'one' to 'access' presence. Neither is there anyone who is needed to dive deeply into some conceptual 'inner body'. Presence is bottomless, and it has neither a body nor a beginning. And It is all there is.

◆   'I am unenlightened', 'I am my ego', and so on and so forth. But something is **knowing** that those thoughts and assumptions are temporarily there. **What** is that something? That is the question that should be centred upon, if you truly want to discover the answer to what you are. It's a magnificent question, because it naturally pauses you. You feel the beauty of its significance, even if the answer to the question remains unclear. The pause is pointing you to your essence, to your own innate clarity and spaciousness. And given that it is innate, it is nothing that you can practise your way to. **You are what you are at this very moment, and you never move from that**, despite any notions otherwise.

◆ No sustained or concentrated efforts are needed for this. You neither have to close your eyes nor move into any kind of special position. For awareness is perfectly present *before* any of those things are done. So why bother? Why waste a millisecond (or a lifetime!) to indulge in any action that is on the mental or physical level? Awareness is neither waiting nor hiding. And there is absolutely nothing to cultivate or to 'bring out'. All of that stuff is just false, spiritual lore. And no matter how tantalizing the stories and anecdotes, they are just experiences, every single one of them.

◆ In spiritual circles, we often hear, 'Who is looking at what?' But it is actually the other way around: '*What* is looking at *who*?' And that 'who' is transitory, imaginary even.

◆ Something is transcending your body, your notions, and your sense of individuality, right at this moment. Again, the transcending is fully occurring. You are *already* over and beyond all of the above. Simply see this for yourself, instead of *attempting* to go beyond your body and mind through some sort of tactic or process.

◆ This understanding can't really be 'developed' or 'surrendered to'. Don't get caught up in these stereotypical aspects of spirituality. Indeed, *non-duality is beyond all spirituality*, because it is speaking about and pointing not only to your natural state, but to Existence itself.

◆ Yes, awareness is subtle. But once it is recognized, you'll wonder how you ever could have missed it. Look right now at this **knowingness** quality within you. **That** is awareness!

◆ There is nothing to extricate and nothing towards which to move. You are what you are at this very second, and you never shift from that. You only **appear** to be your body, emotions, and personality, because you are temporarily identifying with them throughout the day and evening. But you are the existence that is **knowing** that all of those things are briefly appearing.

◆ You aren't your body, your experiences, or even your consciousness. So what is left? What is remaining? You are the pause that you are feeling at this moment. Remain with the pause just long enough to recognize that its stillness and vastness never dissolve. That's all that is needed!

◆ **_Suffering is created through self-identification_**. And self-identification primarily occurs with the body, thoughts/emotions, states of consciousness (I am awake, I am sleepy, I am focused, etc), and—ironically—states of happiness. Regarding the latter, we surmise or are taught that happiness is the greatest thing that we can experience in our day-to-day life. Typically, happiness arises when we get something that we want, or meet a beautiful person, or have some 'spiritual' experience. Then, of course, we not only want to have this moment again, we want to have it permanently! Then we go through decades (or a life-time) of attempting to reach that constant state of happiness. And it's never attained, of course, because **_happiness is an experience: It comes, and it goes. It is not your natural state_**, which is unvarying peace and spaciousness. It's important to be clear on the mechanics of suffering, otherwise, it can continue (though less noticeably) even after the recognition of your natural state.

◆ You are not anything that you can perceive. So right off, you know that you are not your physicality, thoughts, personality, or states of consciousness. So what is left? **_Knowingness_**. Pure Knowingness which presents itself through our body-minds as supreme peace and spaciousness.

◆ The essence of this teaching is this: **You are awareness**. The seeker is just a notion or idea arising **in** that awareness. So take a moment to see what is always present—which is presence itself.

◆ Right at this moment, what is it that your thoughts aren't recognizing? What is it that your thoughts don't know is present? Live with that question throughout the day, if you are drawn to do so, and you just might find the answer that both ordinary seekers and great sages have discovered for themselves.

◆ 'Enlightenment' is always instantaneous. It doesn't piecemeal itself out to you. And why would it? Awareness is without any division whatsoever, and you are that awareness itself. Right at this moment, you **are** That. You aren't this defined person who suddenly (or progressively) 'becomes' your natural identity. So enlightenment is nothing that I can give or offer, because it's your fundamental nature. And you can't **get** what you already **are**! Ponder that statement over and over again. It is one of the golden keys to Self-knowledge.

◆ We're talking about something that is both fully present and is what you are at this very moment. Given that, any kind of action, meditation or practice that would move you 'towards' it, isn't going to work. You will just be moving *away* from it, so to speak. For your idea of 'enlightenment' is very much like a mirage in the desert: Water appears to be directly ahead. But nothing is actually there, except your own *concept* or *notion* about enlightenment!

◆ When you're focused upon a concept or any idea about anything, it's still in the mind. You are merely *thinking* about awareness rather than noticing or understanding its immediate presence. For awareness is more plentiful than all the seas and stars, and yet we miss it.

◆ Life, for 99.99 percent of people, is going from one experience to another. Some experiences are pleasurable, and others aren't. And then there is everything in between. But there is far more to living than this! There is the matter, for one thing, of seeing that your life is *being lived*—and not by this self-important 'you', but by Existence itself. You are a wave on the ocean of limitlessness. Why not see that fully for yourself and have a direct sense of who and what you are? You are the Ocean, you are the Infinitude.

◆ Awareness is what you *are*. You never move away from that. You are the witness to all appearances and to the movement of life. Your thoughts, feelings, sensations, physicalness and consciousness, are all a part of that movement. And anything that changes is an appearance. Therefore, it cannot even begin to be who and what you are. So what is it, right now, that is *not* changing? There is something, at this very moment, that isn't altering in the least. What is it? What is that something? Spend some time with this question. Just sit with it, if you are drawn to do so. And you just may see the answer for yourself—an answer that has always, always been radiantly present.

◆ You are not your body. You are That which is *aware* of your body. What is it, right now, that *knows* that your body and thoughts are present? Remain with the pause that is caused by that question. See that, within the pause, there is a hushed, knowing, *un-altering* presence of peace and spaciousness.

◆ Self-knowledge isn't something that you must 'enter' or 're-enter'. For when do you ever stop being awareness itself?

◆   There is practically no psychological suffering here. Physical ailments—sure: lower back pain, chronic insomnia, teeth/gum issues, and various other middling matters. But my psychological make-up—thoughts, emotions, personality, etc—are seen for what they are: temporary appearances in a true and unconditioned Self.

◆   All beliefs and debates surrounding self-knowledge (whether the perspectives are Buddhist, Zen Buddhist, Taoist, Christian, or non-dual) are operating on a *conceptual* level. And yet, all of the previous frames of spiritual references have their nuggets of truth. They aren't the truths themselves, mind you. They are simply *pointing* to your very own radiance.

◆   It's more about *overlooking* the obvious, rather than being right or wrong. Awareness is what you *are*. Yet, you are scanning the horizons, being captivated by this and that. But however beautiful and tantalizing the sights, thoughts and sensations may be, they pale in comparison to your own innate peace and light. It's boundless and unchanging. And you are precisely That right at this moment. So it's not a matter of your someday '*becoming*' it, or having some grand, visionary experience. There is nothing to attain or even hope for! But just to be clear, it's fine to want and earnestly explore this understanding. Just be mindful of the point that you are wanting something that you absolutely presently *are*.

◆ Forget about tomorrow. Tomorrow is a thought. It's the mind and 'me' in full operation. What is it *right now* that is utterly hushed, unvarying, and clarity itself?

◆ On the table sits a small Buddha. The Buddha is compact and gilded, with numinous, half-closed eyes. Seekers sit this way in hopes of reaching their own transcendence, not realizing that it is the other way around: You *first* see or understand that you *are* Transcendence.

◆ If the mind could show you your actual Self, you would have seen it by now.

◆ What is it, that does not know your name?

◆ This understanding isn't gradual. Yes, issues may be clarified over one's lifetime. But there is no maturation on the part of presence. What does appear to occur, however, is a deep recognition that experiences are transitory. Thus, you are likely to find yourself savouring a moment while, at the same time, letting it go. Or rather, there is the understanding that it is fleeting. There is no one there to *let* it go! It's a kind of deep appreciation of things, without any grasping.

◆ Right at this moment, what is the presence that your mind and thoughts aren't creating?

◆ You can't even **be** what you are. For you already **are** what you are! And your inherent nature **does not change**.

◆ Your own direct experience of what you are is what frees you from the notion, that something needs to be done to grasp or garner liberation. Your very nature is 100% liberated! Even individualistic thoughts about yourself can't suppress the Self in any form, shape, or manner.

◆ Any action towards awareness is just idiotic.

◆ The thought, 'I am bounded', is silly, and the thought, 'I am Freedom', is redundant, even though it is pointing to the truth. The thing to see here is that **you are not your thoughts** at all!

◆ So long as you feel that you have to 'get enlightened', you are **anticipating**: You are mentally projecting what has **already** taken place. You **are** pure awareness at this very moment. So what is there to be done? **Who** wants to do **what**? And **why**? You are operating solely on procedural and conceptual levels when there is a 'who' that wants to do this.

◆   This understanding isn't some higher level of consciousness or anything like that. Consciousness remains pretty much the same, and awareness is totally beyond it, as I've said any number of times here. So any activity or practice that promises 'advanced' levels of alertness and knowingness is still on the level of the mind, no matter how many psychic or expansive experiences you may have.

◆ The mind and practices can't possibly bring you lasting peace. The mind and certain yoga practices, for instance, certainly have their place. And I don't want to sound as if I am totally discounting them, because I am not. I'm merely saying that true peace and clarity comes with the recognition of your immediate presence-awareness.

◆   Fundamentally, you are simply your nature—pure awareness. This is your abiding reality, this is what never changes. Everything else is just transitional appearances, from your body and personality to your brain and consciousness. If you were just any of those things, you wouldn't have the ability to know it. No self-reflection would be possible.

◆   Just remain with that empty, aware luminosity. Or rather, see that you actually never move from it, that it is always there, whether your attention goes to your coffee cup or to the clarity.

◆ Metaphysical exercises are just as non-productive for self-realization as practices and disciplines. But if you are drawn to explore these things, by all means do so. Enjoy your life. And perhaps one day, you will see that liberating methods don't liberate.

◆ Take a moment to see what has always, always been present. You are placing all of your emphasis on your mind, and the mind really isn't the issue. *You are focusing on the wrong thing*. All spiritual seekers the world over are focusing on the wrong thing. Your mind (if it is neurologically sound and sane) is, in all probability, working normally. Rising thoughts and emotions are a part of your functioning. You simply are not seeing that not only is awareness fully present, but that it never moves from being so.

◆ Thoughts and feelings come and go. But something doesn't. What is that something?

◆ Yes, we are all One. But what *is* that Oneness? What is that singularity that is in each transitional body and mind? You see, if you merely *say* that we are all One, it's theoretical. You are just throwing words around. But when you actually attempt to see and understand that magnificent principle that is within each of us, then it becomes an engaging and energetic investigation.

◆ You don't need to *try* to step out of the 'stream of thinking'. You're *already* out! You are continuing to believe in the assumption that you are the thinker, when you're employing some practice or effort to step out of the stream. Again, you're *already* out! Thoughts happen *in* you, not *to* you!

◆ *You never move from being absolute awareness: That is the ultimate truth*. That is a pointer that pauses you because of its pronounced clarity and simplicity. Reflect upon that truth throughout the day, if you're moved to do so. 'I am awareness. I never move from this. There is nothing to get, because *I am That already: absolute awareness*.' Don't make it mechanical or even contemplative! Just see the actuality to which the words are pointing.

◆ You are the presence that is *already* beyond all thinking. Now when I say 'beyond', I obviously don't mean that it is something that you haven't yet gotten. I also don't mean that you have to somehow ascend to it or to go in some direction towards it.

◆ Yes, you have to see your self for yourself. But that self couldn't see easier, I promise you. It only *appears* tricky, because you are awareness *already*. So there is nothing to see as an object. All that you can do (or that is needed) is the *recognition* of your own presence of peace and spaciousness. That is all.

◆ Additional readings of non-dual books, blogs and web-sights can be immensely helpful in getting a handle on your true nature, especially if those works are pointing **beyond** the page and computer screen. For one of the many glories of this teaching is that it is directing you to what you are **at this very moment**, and not to some mystical experience or 'attainable' state. You **are** awareness **already**. So there is nothing to attain. So as you continue to read, keep in mind that the answer is within **you** and not within the words. What you're looking for is a hushed and undeniable presence of peace and spaciousness. That's it.

◆ Your true nature has to be something that **never** varies in the least. Reflecting upon that truth, you may be significantly paused. The mind stops. Then awareness— in the form of serenity and expansiveness—is recognized, and is immediately understood as having **always** been present.

◆ With a little clear seeing, you will be able to recognize that this natural state of yours is—as the words indicate— naturally and fully present.

◆ '*What is it that knows these thoughts?*': Let go of the question and bring your attention to the pause. As long as you are centred on the question, you are immersed in thought. You are remaining on a conceptual level. But you are the pause, you see. *You Are The Pause*. That 'changeless space' *is* you. And that changeless space is no void. It only appears so at first glance. But its depth is immeasurable, and it is replete with peace and plenitude. Just a slight conceptual 'relaxation' is all that is needed. And then all will be made clear.

◆ Self-knowledge cannot be practised. The understanding is either there or it isn't.

◆ What is it that you are not moving from?... What we want to be alert for is the presence of what appears to be ordinary stillness. Then take a timeless moment to notice that that stillness actually never moves. It is immeasurable and beginningless. And it is your true self.

◆ What is the presence of awareness that is present right now, as you carefully read these words?... Again, what, *really,* is the presence of awareness that is present *right now*, as you slowly peruse these words?

◆ There is, of course, no place where awareness is not. So the only pilgrimage that needs to be made is an inner one, and that automatically occurs when you naturally and knowingly come to a full conceptual stop.

◆ There can be no 'progressive dismantling' of the ego. It may seemingly take some time to directly see this for yourself. But the issue of the ego not being a defined entity (but rather the recurring sense-of-self) can be recognized at any moment. No specific duration is needed. Because you think time is required to do the dismantling, you are giving undue credence to it and to a fictional ego, both of which are not a factor in your understanding.

◆ What you are *is* the natural state, which is utter peace and serenity. There is no 'one' there to 'accept' anything! It *is* you. So there is nothing for you to do except recognize that, right here and now, you are awareness itself: **You never move from that**. You absolutely never move from that. Contemplate this fact, with ease and naturalness, and all will be seen clearly.

◆   Your own inner stillness is the answer which you are seeking. *That* is it. You feel that stillness any number of times throughout the day, but you give it very little heed or attention (not that it requires effort or concentration to discover). The next time you are paused by a passage in a book or a nature scene or by someone's beauty or kindness, stay with the pause just long enough to see that you actually never move from that pause!

◆   Freedom is recognizing that you are freedom itself. You don't have to **become** free from a single thing. That perceived individual that you take yourself to be is merely a concept that you have about yourself. But **before** that thought about yourself arises, what is it that is *already* there? Not *who*, but *what*. Just sit with that for a few moments, for it points to your very essence: not *who*, but *what*.

◆   To think of yourself as a 'divine being' still entails an imagined separation from awareness. Just keep coming back to the point of awareness being all that that 'divine being' is, and that you *are* that—or rather, *That*, as the sages orate. And even 'That' is merely a term pointing to what you are, to your natural state.

◆　　There is no 'shift' to the immeasurable. It's simply a matter of discovering, instantly and unequivocally, that awareness has always been fully present, and that you *are* that presence. And when you see this for yourself, it will be as clear and as evident to you as your own breathing.

◆　　The map isn't the territory, and neither is any expression about your natural state. Presence is what you *are*, and the word is merely directing you to that fact. So allow your attention to follow the direction in which the descriptions and expressions are pointing. And you just may find clarity itself.

◆　　You not only never move from being what you are, *you never move*—period! Remain with the pause that that pointer instills. You are That which never alters in the least! So the recognition of this natural state of yours is simply a matter of discerning what it is, right here and now, *That Is Not Moving*.

◆　　Yes, there is something that isn't moving in the least. Yet, it is immeasurable and fully present. What *is* that something?... Well, *you* are that something. And if you are that something (i.e. awareness) at this very moment, your not recognizing it must mean that you are merely *overlooking* it. It is that simple.

◆ There is no relationship between objects and awareness, however 'intimate' that relationship may be. For all things *are* awareness, even the appearances. And we want to give those appearances due significance, rather than no significance at all. For we want to be able to go to the grocery store and interact with others as smoothly and as safely as possible, while understanding that, fundamentally, there is nothing that is *not* awareness.

◆ You don't have to try to stop thought or watch thoughts in order to snatch, gain, or merge with awareness. Just see that awareness is never not present. Stay with that fact: *Awareness Is Never Not Present*! And you are That, awareness itself!

◆ Awareness can neither be acquired nor avoided.

◆ You are already what you are seeking. There's nothing hindering you from being what you are right now. And what you are right now is awareness itself. When that fact is seen or realized, your identity will be clear. There is no practice or process that 'catapults' you to presence because, once again, presence is your natural state. So nothing can 'speed up' the process because you are *already* That. Thus, there is no process! It's just a matter of seeing or understanding this for yourself, which, of course, not only can happen at any moment, but which takes less than a moment to realize.

◆ The natural state is a hushed background of peace and spaciousness. And yes, it's there all the time, whether I'm noticing it or not. Thoughts and feelings arise and fall, but Presence is ever-present. Other teachers and writers may describe it differently, but for me the above words come closest to what I'm experiencing.

◆ Just be mindful that credible books, blogs, writings, and teachers, are always pointing **beyond** themselves to the reader's or listener's own innate freedom.

◆ You aren't trying to 'get' anything. You are merely recognizing something that has never not been directly in front of you.

◆ What is it, right now, that you do **not** have to attain?

◆ You say that you are trying to 'reach' or 'merge with' the Absolute. But awareness-presence **is** the Absolute. And it is the only thing there is! **The seeker is an idea, a notion, a falsehood**. It has to be seen through or understood in order for self-realization to occur.

◆ What is present **before** your next thought is present?

◆ 'Who am I?' is the wrong question. You're not a **who**. You are a **what**.

◆   Again, you cannot 'free the mind from thinking'. That is just utter nonsense. I don't care how lovely or spiritual it sounds. That is not going to happen—until you are dead or in some profound coma of some kind. And it's all beside the point anyway. For the mind momentarily and automatically frees itself from thoughts on a continual basis. For no thought is actually connected to another thought anyway. *There is a natural space between each thought, and you are that space*.

◆   There *is* no individual to 'stay in the present moment'. What is going to happen is that a thought or feeling or sensation is going to arise in that moment, and you are going to assume that it is you. But you—your true self—*are* that moment. You're the witness, *not* the manifestation. You are the knowing spaciousness that heretofore has been overlooked.

◆   The 'play of life' is actually the play of appearances— things that seem to exist for a certain while and then disappear (whether that duration is a nanosecond or 10 billion years). But anything that has a beginning and an end cannot, *under any circumstances*, be who or what you are. Remain mindful of that fact as you go about your daily activities, or when you want to sit in contemplation of some non-dual issue.

◆ *Self-realization is about 'seeing' and 'understanding', not 'doing'*. Awareness is totally beyond all causality. Totally! So how can any action or ritual or practice take you there? If I could give you a glimpse—from my vantage point—on the complete non-relationship between awareness and practices, you would roar with laughter at your own actions. But then, a glimpse is all you would need to see and understand that Presence is your natural state.

◆ Thoughts have no inherent intelligence. They arise and fall within a kind of supreme intelligence (awareness). And we are *That*. We are *not* our thoughts. Thoughts have no cognitizing power of their own. They are mental appearances, though they can be memory-like, musical-like, and picture-like. Some neuroscientists say that thoughts are merely separate, neurochemical reactions. That's fine too. However you label them, they are vital to our living responsibly and communicating effectively.

◆ Right now, there is something about you that isn't moving in the least. What is that something?... You are the pause that just answered that question. Just relax and see the ease and magnificence to this: *You* are the pause that answered that question!

◆ If you were in deep sleep right now, there is something from your waking state that would still be present. What is that something?

◆ The seeker is imagined. The sought is *already* present.

◆ *Who* is doing *what*? You see, that's the question that should naturally arise when you are engaged in any sort of practice or technique to 'achieve' enlightenment or whatever you want to call it. *'Who' is doing 'what'?* The question should come up, because you are utilizing two notions or appearances—a perceived individual and an action 'towards' something—that have nothing whatsoever to do with self-realization! Nothing! So how on earth are they going to launch you into this final understanding? The only way such an understanding is going to occur is when, while doing them, you see their futility and simply stop! (as the Buddha did.)

◆ Everyone is *looking*, but few are actually *seeing*. But that lack of recognition is due, in large part, to the obviousness of awareness, and not to its obscurity.

◆ Gaze into your own emptiness. And by 'gaze' I mean to simply take a calm and direct look at it. If you do it just right, you will see a presence of peace and expansiveness that you have simply neglected to notice up to now. Further, that presence, once fully discerned, never disappears—whether you are raking the leaves, having a disagreement with your partner, or enjoying a cup of tea or coffee. In a word, take a look at that which is never lost.

◆ How can you 'journey' to what you already *are*? That pointer stops you cold. Or rather, it halts the mind from thinking that I must '*do*' something in order to '*get*' enlightenment.

◆ At this particular moment, what is it that is knowing that your body is present? And again, that is a *what* and not a *who*. And that *what-ness* appears as, among other things, unchanging peace and spaciousness. You can't even say that it is teeming with space and equanimity, because those are quantifiable terms. And *your natural state is wholly without measure*. Just a little clear-seeing here is all that is needed.

◆ Only the mind, ego or sense-of-self causes you to think that a process or practice is needed for self-realization. But nothing could be further from the truth, literally speaking. This understanding comes suddenly and quietly, though it may occur in the most frantic of times and places. And no preparation, duties or code of morals are necessary for the seeing. And why would there be? For you are what you are, as you read these words. And what you are is nothing less than awareness itself.

◆   Only a 'who' can attempt to meditate. But no 'success' can occur there, because a 'who' (an assumed person or meditator) cannot awaken. Why? Because the 'who' is a thought and a concept. And a thought cannot awaken. Further, thoughts are not your fundamental reality—awareness is. So the moment you attempt to meditate or practise any kind of mindfulness, you move *away* from presence! You move *away* from the very thing that you are seeking! Thus, as Ramana Maharshi rightly noted, 'your very effort is bondage'.

◆   What is it that you aren't seeing?... Let this be the question that you reflect upon throughout the day or evening, whenever the question naturally arises... What is it that you are *not* seeing? The question pauses you, and you are the pause—the Eternal Pause that is without beginning or end. And that pause is never not there... What is it that you are not seeing?...

◆   Coming to this understanding involves no movement whatsoever. You are merely seeing what you always have been: your ordinary, everyday awareness. You just haven't noticed its fullness and actuality—indeed, its *extra*-ordinariness. And there is nothing that needs to be watched, purified, perfected, or attained. You are *not* your body or your thoughts. You are that which is *aware* of your body and your thoughts.

133

◆ If you are aware of something as an object (your physicality, your thoughts, your feelings, etc), then you can't possibly **be** that. Therefore, you must be that which is **knowing** that those things are making an appearance. So what is this **knowing-ness** that I am failing to see, though it is directly before and within me? It has to be my true nature. It has to be what I **am**, what I absolutely never move away from!

◆ The question is, 'What **is** that awareness?' But you have to be careful with all of this, for you don't want to remain with that question stringently. If you do, you're keeping it on a mindful and therefore conceptual level. Just forget the word 'awareness' itself and focus on this innate presence of serenity and spaciousness that is directly within and before you. And I assure you, it is absolutely there for the seeing and understanding. And you never move away from this. And why would you? It's your nature!

◆ *Q: In my email correspondence with John Wheeler, he kept pointing again and again to my true nature, encouraging me to actually **see** what that is, rather than just giving it a name or using words, which I had been quite prone to do up to that point.*

Rodney: Yes, the automatic labelling, and then remaining with that conceptual handle, instead of simply seeing your own immediacy.

134

*Q: Before truly looking into the nature of my being, I believed that thoughts would somehow have to die down or lose their intensity for this truth to be realized. I held onto this notion until John Wheeler pointed out that 'thoughts are not and never have been the problem'. This was good news, indeed! But the real death rattle for this assumed separate self came when John asked, 'What would be driving the need or interest in identification in the first place?' This paused me completely. Then, suddenly, it became crystal clear to me that all of 'my' seeking and suffering was based on a false premise: There is absolutely no separate entity cut off from life, but rather, just life itself, in all its freedom and functioning through all apparent forms! I found that I had been seeking my very own nature—this limitless source of peace and spaciousness—the whole time. It had **always** been there; I had just been overlooking it! But now, there is just pure seeing, knowing and being—no more doubts, problems, or mental suffering. This natural state of ours is just indescribable, yet very ordinary. It is present prior to all appearances. Completely obvious. Incredibly simple. And always shining.*

◆ The 'I' is an idea and a convenience. It allows us to communicate with one another and to function in society. But this 'I' is not your true identity. You are the serene and unchanging spaciousness **behind** the 'I'. See for yourself that there is indeed something behind and around that notion of a concrete 'me'. It may appear intangible and ambiguous. But that 'something' is present nonetheless.

◆ This understanding is a kind of hushed astonishment.

◆ You have to see the simplicity of this—the simplicity of what you are, right here and now. It isn't a question of your coming to this understanding at some later time when you are 'spiritually ready', or when you can 'give time' to some sort of quest or search. Those are blinders and postponements that the mind is creating. **The mind has nothing to do with the reality of what you are**, as you read these very words. So **who** is waiting for **what**?... Feel the pause and power of that pointer. Allow it to show you the tranquil and unmoving immediacy of your natural state.

◆　There is nothing to 'detect'. You are simply recognizing a presence that has *always* been present. And that presence is pure awareness, which is what each of us is. And given that that is a fact, there is, then, no 'each of us': *Everything* is awareness. Our bodies, thoughts, states of consciousness, and universe, are appearances *in* that awareness. Though the appearances have a certain reality, a body or a mind (just to use two examples) can't possibly be who and what we are because, among other things, they are transitory, they have no inherent intelligence, and they are *being perceived*.

◆　'Enlightenment' is fully present as your ordinary awareness. That is the understanding to which the true sages are pointing, and which Nisargadatta Maharaj was highlighting in nearly all of his talks. So come back to what you *are*, at this very moment. The answer is right there, and it has never moved from being there.

◆　Your unconditional freedom is what you are *right now*, which is pure awareness. Nothing needs to be done other than to see that this is a fact. Indeed, your doing and practices *postpone* your seeing this fact. Your actions are getting in the way of your realizing what is directly before you. So just take a calm breath, have a cup of coffee or tea, and just sit with these pointers. Allow them to direct you to what is immediately available.

◆ **_There is no causation in transcendence_**. You do not perform a certain *asana* or engage in a particular meditative practice for x number of minutes, and then this understanding occurs. Your natural state is there even **before** either of those actions are done or even thought about!

◆ Transcendental meditation and mindfulness may help you to lower your blood pressure and superficial levels of stress, but they do not lead to self-realization. The latter is a deep understanding and recognition of your natural state. With that said, enjoy TM and mindfulness, if you like. Ditto any form of meditation. Enjoy what you enjoy!

◆ The question that spiritual seekers are quick to ask is, 'How do I meditate?' But a deeper and more fundamental question is, 'How do I bypass meditation altogether?' Or even better, 'How do I discover that my natural state has nothing to do with meditation whatsoever?' You are pure awareness **_at this moment_**. So any pursuant activity after the fact is simply ludicrous.

◆ There is no need to bring 'unity to diversity'. For there **_is_** no actual diversity.

◆ When you make any attempt to reach or acquire that ever-present Immovable by, say, slowing the mind or watching your thoughts, you don't get a single step closer to it, because the mind, the thoughts, and the determined watcher, are *not* part of presence, of the Immovable. They are just ephemeral clouds *within* it. In fact, there is no getting from one to the other! The real sky is completely beyond anything that arises within it. Further, you are sky *already*! You *are* the spaciousness and the freedom. So there is nothing that you can *get*. There is a spaciousness within you, at this very moment, and you are looking everywhere but there. What and where is that spaciousness? You see, that question directs you to a stillness to which you have given very little attention.

◆ *You and awareness are the very same thing*. This fact is simply not being recognized.

◆ Think of awareness as consciousness without movement, that is, consciousness without thoughts, emotions, memories, or any notions of yesterday, tomorrow, and even the present. Although that is a rough approximation of presence, it may help you to discern what is being pointed to, which is a felt, aware stillness.

◆ Any deeds to directly 'reach' or 'attain' enlightenment (such as affirmations or visualisations) are doomed to failure. Just rest assured that self-knowing is far simpler than engaging in any of those activities. Far simpler. Even as we are talking right now, *you are already what you are seeking*. Awareness is what you *are*. Yet, you are *seeking* awareness!... I say that not to chastise you, but to help you to see the beauty and the simplicity of non-dual inquiry.

◆ *Stillness is the door to the eternal*.

◆ Stillness cannot be cultivated. It can only be understood by *recognizing* it.

◆ *Your essence is wholly non-dual*. It is not even oneness, but rather a '*what-ness*' that never alters in the least. Awakening to this reality is merely a matter of noticing what it is about you that is always present, that is always the same. There is a very real constant within you, and nothing could be more tranquil or exquisite.

◆   If you have the idea of being 'unliberated' or 'unenlightened', you are bound by that notion, by that particular illusion. Your belief essentially stops you from seeing what is unconditionally present, right here and now. But it is just belief. That is all. It has nothing whatsoever to do with your actually being awareness itself. Also, a thought or idea is just a fleeting appearance *in* awareness. So don't sell yourself short. That belief can be gone in an inkling with just a bit of careful investigation and seeing. When no self-identification is there, what is present, what is still remaining? Awareness itself. It is *never not present*, of course. It is merely being *overlooked*.

◆   Why are you attempting to soar and be 'transcendent', when you are *already* the sky?

◆   'Awakening' and 'enlightenment' are concepts themselves. For you *are* unlimited freedom, even as you read these words. You do not become 'freer' when this understanding occurs. You simply realize that awareness is your essence, and that it was never lost to you.

◆   *Your own presence is the key to self-knowing*. But you habitually think of this presence as your body, thoughts, feelings, and sensations. But I am speaking of a non altering *This-ness* that is there *before* any thoughts or sensations arise.

◆ If a mistaken idea or conviction is the only thing keeping you from self-realization, how is any meditation or activity going to help you? You are squarely in depths of the most magnificent of oceans, and yet you are begging to see water. I could easily say, 'Choose any direction!' And I would be right. But you see, you do not even have to do that—to position yourself in any particular way. And neither do you have to get into a specific *asana* or make any preparatory gestures. All that is necessary is to simply perceive that not only are you **already** in the ocean, but that you are the very sea *itself*.

◆ You can see the truth of those words at this very moment. Any notions of your having to do something at some later time gives credence to the conviction that self-knowing is time-dependent. So, try shifting your view from 'I am not awakened' to 'I am not my body or my mind: I am awareness itself! What is it that I am **not** seeing?' Those are still thoughts, of course. But see if you can see and feel the stillness to which they are pointing.

◆   What you are at this moment is the solution to all of this. Awareness is fully and unequivocally present, and you *are* that awareness. Merely see that this is the case. What is it that is being disregarded? What is it, right here and now, that is closer than your very own breathing, and yet is not being recognized? It is not your body, or your thoughts, or your personality, or your changing states of consciousness. So what does that leave you with?

◆   See through all self-identification, whether it is through the notion of your being a man, woman, spiritual person, enlightened, unenlightened, non-dualist—you name it. Something is existing that is wholly *beyond* any of those categories. And allow that clarification to be swift, natural, and enlivening. Don't be overly demanding with yourself about this. For that would be the subtle 'me' in operation.

◆   You cannot 'relax into awareness'. The former is an action, and the latter an abiding reality. And because it is abiding, there is never a time when it is absent. Also, because awareness is all there is, just *who* would be 'relaxing' his or her way into it?

◆ Any time you bring 'Who?', 'When?' and 'How?' into a non-duality discussion, you are muddling things up. You are also being nonsensical. Those things are just not a factor in the direct recognition of your natural state. They may have a place in general spirituality discussions (though that could certainly be debated!). But if your interest is in the *immediate* understanding of who and what you are, theological discourses will hold little or no appeal for you.

◆ We habitually associate experiences with points of self-reference. We feel that they define us, and that our fundamental reality is somehow made up of those experiences. But experiences that occur happen *in* awareness. They appear and disappear, and never touch or interact with presence-awareness.

◆ Consciousness is a *state* of awareness as well as an *appearance*. It is not awareness itself. It appears in varying states, because it is directly tied to the alertness and functioning of our body (its sleep, deep sleep, drowsiness, awakeness, etc). On the other hand, awareness radiates *through* consciousness, so to speak. It is self-shining and never alters in the least.

◆ Consciousness and sentience, while vital to our humanness, are changeable. Therefore they are experiences and cannot be who and what we fundamentally are.

◆ The 'doer' is a concept as well as a mistaken notion. If you look carefully, you will observe that, for the most part, there are only thoughts and observations, followed by feelings and actions. Indeed, you don't even know what your next thought will be! What is apparent, then, is that *you are the witness to all of this, not the initiator or the driver*. When this understanding dawns on you, living becomes like a near-effortless balancing act with no signs of a juggler.

◆ You are striving for this so-called enlightenment. But the meditator, the striving, and this enlightenment, are all notions and actions that are getting in your way. They are *preventing* you from seeing what is *already* directly within you: your unvarying presence of unblemished awareness. That is what you *are*, and that is what needs to be perceived and understood. All else are just half-measures and fantastical thinking.

◆ Again, it all comes down to the pointing *beyond* the inherent conceptual limitations. For one of the first things you are going to realize when you come to this understanding yourself is how *simple* it is to recognize your true being, and how no technique can possibly 'take' you to this.

◆   You are awareness itself, which means that you are the answer to the question *at this very moment*. There is nothing really to sort—only to *see*. It's a clarification, more than anything else. And nothing could be easier.

◆   *Any true spiritual awakening is simply the recognition of your natural and ever-present being*.

◆   *Q*: *We are so used to this thing called 'mind', that most of the time we don't even realize it is chattering away at us. When we do notice it, it is usually when it gets so busy in there, so loud and bothersome, that we just wish it would shut up with its judging, comparing, calculating and strategizing.*

Rodney: The mind is quiet more often than we realize. And if you could simply notice when those actions appear and see them for what they are, then the mind isn't a problem. You see, a thought—by its very nature—is dualistic. It is saying that there is 'someone' there who is judging or calculating. But in actuality, there is only that particular thought arising in that particular brain and body. You, fundamentally, are not the thought, body, brain, or consciousness (which constitutes the changes in your alertness, such as being awake, asleep, drowsy, dreaming, etc). You are that which is *aware* of them.

Q: *Yes, I suppose the mind stops more often than we notice. But we are so used to it being around, so used to its endless commentary and its enormous facility when it comes to analyzing and announcing the news, that we fail to observe the quiet within us. In fact, if we do notice the quiet at all, we are bothered by it. We actually want the commentary to continue. It's a little like being around someone very annoying for a long time. We wish they would go away, but then when they do, we realize how much we miss them.*

Rodney: As long as you are alive and healthy, you are going to have thoughts. And I'm confident that you would rather have them than not! And who wants to be around annoying people?! But the bottom line here is that there simply *is* no mind: The mind is a concept, an idea. There are only thoughts which—when they appear—we label as 'the mind'. And thoughts are basically four things: memory, imagination, reasoning (that occurs via the brain), and neurological responses to your surroundings.

Q: *And the search for enlightenment can easily be understood to be deeply involved in this so-called 'mind' issue.*

Rodney: Right, because run-of-the-mill seekers assume that there is a division between them and the thing that they are seeking, and so they want to make strides 'towards' self-realization. And then there are those hardcore spiritual foragers who either want to eradicate the ego or still the mind completely. And neither of this is going to happen. Forget it! That is just yogic and metaphysical lore. Still, people are going on expensive, faraway retreats and *satsangs* to do all of the above. When I meet or talk with these people, I tend to get this sudden 'flash' of the rest of their lives. Twenty years from now, say, they will either have ceased all meditating out of blighted frustration, or they will be soldiering on, with some sort of nonsensical 'happy' face. And that is the place where 99% of the spiritual seekers are (and that's a conservative estimate, by the way!).

Q: *Thank goodness there are a few credible teachers like yourself, John Wheeler, and Bob Adamson, who are saying that there really is no enlightenment—that, if anything, we are* **already** *enlightened! That there is nothing to do, nowhere to go, nothing to accomplish.*

Rodney: Well, one could argue that there **is** something to be done. But that is merely the recognition that what you are searching for is **already** present—**fully** present, in fact. And that you **are** That. And this understanding occurs on its own. There is no 'you' to do anything at all. Further, that recognition is neither progressive nor time-dependent. It all churns down to the fact that you are awareness itself. You always were and you always will be.

Q: And once this is recognized, you will find that there is this subtle feeling of spaciousness there, perhaps even a bit of serenity, correct?

Rodney: A serene spaciousness is certainly an apt description of it.

Q: And the more time you spend there, the more you will begin to see that it's more than just quietness. It's downright silent. And if you remain even longer, you may begin to see that there is actually no subject, no object. The field and the trees are still there, and you are clearly here in the chair looking out, but—try as you may—you will soon see that there is really no one here. Literally no one. Then you realize that this is really more peaceful than you thought at first. It is actually quite wonderful, but in a very quiet way.

Rodney: Right, there is a definite hushness to the immeasurableness. But awareness isn't directional: You are not seeing the fields and trees in a specific manner. They are simply appearances in this unvarying space of peace and boundlessness. Also, once Presence is seen and understood, that is it. You cannot directly explore it, **because there is no one to do so**! And there are no 'deeper' or 'more peaceful' areas to it: It is all one vastness.

Q: Well, this is surely the 'enlightenment' that everyone is looking for, the one that was here all along. It is the space *in which the noisy mind appears. It is the Thing/Non-thing that the teachers have been talking about. And it's not only completely and totally yours, but it **is** you.*

Rodney: Exactly. It is not yours, but **you**! There is no individual to own or obtain it. All there is is a sense of fleeting and frequent individuality. Your natural state is that in which nothing changes in the least. And you can discern that truth and reality right now, if you were to take a close and careful look at what is being said here. But don't simply remain with the words. **See** what it is, **within** you, that the words are **pointing** to. You are your very own treasure trove, and it is all there for the having!

◆   The true nature of the mind can never be understood by the mind. So how do you think it is going to help you with recognizing your natural state?

◆   There is no separation between you and what you are seeking. Feel the significance of these words. Allow whatever pause that occurs to occur. Remain with it. Feel its depth, peace, and actuality. This is **you**—your verifiable and unwavering state. Go back to the original sentence, if necessary, in a natural and inquisitive way. Again, **there is no separation between you and what you are seeking**.

◆ *What is it that is always present and that never changes in the least?*

◆ In reality, awareness is not even the ground or the substratum of existence, because there *is* nothing but awareness!

◆ There is no relationship between awareness and your thoughts and feelings. None whatsoever. They actually do not arise from nor disappear into awareness. They are merely appearances *in* it. They have no weight or substance. They are fleeting practicalities to help us to function smoothly in our lived lives.

◆ *There is only perception, no perceiver.* See how this is going on throughout the day. There is constant perceiving—visually, aurally, physically, etc. Occasionally, a thought or an emotion will appear, and we automatically think that that is 'me' thinking or feeling. But thoughts and feelings are just evanescent flashings in this vastness of perception.

◆   Awareness never appears and departs—indeed, it never alters in the least! Its main attributes (when it manifests through the body and consciousness) are utter peace and spaciousness. There is clarity too, of course, but it is more of an understanding that you *are* this serenity and infinitude. Further, thoughts continue, but there is the clear realization that any temporary identification with your thoughts and body is no big deal. Indeed, that fleeting association allows you to function in society! As for inner joy? I suppose so. But even that is a stretch. For there is really no emotional component to this understanding at all.

◆ What is it, at this moment, that is devoid of all emotions, characteristics, and limitations? You are that which is quite distinct from any phenomenal characteristics. Can you zero in on what precisely '*that*' is? It is subtle, but ever-present. And once recognized, it is never lost.

◆ Why are you so fascinated with practices? Why can't you simply live a full and congenial life from your eternal source of presence? No practice is going to take you to that fullness. Indeed, the practice is going to do the direct opposite. It focuses your life on actions and ideas, rather than on your natural and non-moving state. But no, you opt for the ever-exhausting mirage of 'Enlightenment'. But let me be clear: I am not saying that self-realization isn't a fact. Because it most certainly is. What I'm saying is that you cannot come to self-knowledge through methods and techniques. And anyone who says as much needs to have their medication adjusted.

◆ Philosophical discussions are fine to a point. But after a while, the shallowness of such conversations becomes woefully apparent. You soon find yourself wanting to know the actual vastness *beyond* the verbiage. That is certainly what *I* wanted! What is that sublimity that 'passes all understanding'? How can I know it as solidly as my own breathing? That is what brought me this 'final' understanding.

◆ Don't leave things at a conceptual level if you want to make any headway with self-knowledge. Insights are fine and welcomed. But what are the insights and perceptions pointing *to*?

◆ The person imagines him- or herself to be a defined and separate entity through assumptions and unexamined responses to the environment.

◆ There *seem* to be cause and effect because there *seem* to be individual people and objects in everyday life. Presence, however, is completely beyond these occurrences. But this can only be understood *after* the recognition of your own, actual nature as pure awareness. Then you will see that cause and effect are just everyday appearances in your infinite vastness.

◆ Awareness doesn't need to be 'awakened'. It is there for the seeing and the understanding. A simple recognition is all that is required. And that recognition is dependent upon neither methods nor morals. Also, no defined or individual person 'awakens'. It is simply a case of awareness discovering itself, which can occur along with the appearance of body and consciousness.

◆ To concentrate or meditate on a stillness that somehow must be 'attained' is a gross inaccuracy which will not help you in the least with true self-knowing. To 'turn your attention inwards' means to take note of a supreme and inner peace that is simply being *overlooked*. That is all.

◆ You don't have to perform a single chant or ritual to bring forth your true nature, since it is your natural state already. Chant for the beauty of chanting. The same applies to yoga and meditation: Do them for the benefits they bring, or simply for the pleasure of doing them. Your natural state is *already* fully present. So *what* is it that you are *not* seeing?

◆ There are two central points to keep in mind: You are *not* your thoughts and feelings, and presence is *always* and *unconditionally* present. Even more, it is precisely what never changes. And you are that right now – you *are* that awareness. So it is merely a matter of noticing a perpetual presence of peace, quietude, and limitlessness. And it's there for the seeing. Indeed, *it is never not there*!

◆ Just be mindful that we are talking about your *natural* state here. So it is something that you are existing as *at this moment*. Nothing is being 'attained' or 'merged with'. Neither are you 'absorbed into' anything. All of that is just spiritual gobbledygook. For none of that gets to the essential question, 'Who is the knower?', which is the query that occupies the more discerning seeker. However, *there is no 'who', only a 'what'*. And that *what-ness* is awareness proper. Sit with this, ponder it, and walk with it, if necessary, but all in a natural and reflective manner. And that will lead you to the answer that you presently *are*.

◆ Our attention routinely goes to our bodies, sensations, emotions, and beliefs. And that's okay for our everyday life. But for self-knowing a more careful and deliberate kind of looking is required. And yet, it takes just a moment to recognize your self-knowing nature. Or even less so!

◆ Your own ever-present awareness is the teaching.

◆ What is your state *before* any thought arises, *before* any question is asked? Look into this with calmness and clarity, and clarity itself will be your answer.

◆ The closest a thought or expression can come to this understanding is, '*I am*'.

◆ It's really funny to see how non-existent this personal 'I' or self actually is. **We are taking an appearance and recurring function to be what we are**. That is why some of the great Zen masters laughed when they become self-realized themselves. I continue to find myself chuckling, even years after having come to this understanding.

◆ There is really no future attainment or great event. You need to look at what you are *right at this moment*. That is where the answer lies. You are existing as awareness *as we speak*, and that fact merely has to be recognized. It is nothing remote at all.

◆ Practices aim at getting results. And because results would be something different from what you are right now, practices are inherently counter-productive.

◆ What is *already* free and *completely* present?

◆ When you come to this understanding, you shouldn't have a single question left. Not one!

◆ Something is *prior* to thought. Can you take note of precisely what that is? It's there for the seeing and recognizing at this very moment. Again, something is present *prior* to any thought or feeling. What is that something?

◆ My books and blog are just pointers to something that is always present. They are reminders that something is being overlooked. So, in actuality, you end up discovering all of this for yourself, and by yourself. No one can hand or 'transmit' this understanding to you. And give no heed to anyone who claims that they can. If you are awareness already, how can they possibly transfer awareness to you? So be wary of those who are overly spiritual, because there is absolutely nothing spiritual about this. *Your natural state is beyond all spirituality*. Presence is over and above rituals, ceremonies, temples, and churches. Awareness is present just as fully in India as it is in any other location in the world. The place is incidental. But *you* are not.

◆   Knowing that you are nothing, and yet everything, is beyond any words that you could say about it. I mean, why even try to describe the feeling. It is nothing that you can adequately capture.

◆   *Who* is looking for *what*? There is no 'who' : Awareness is all there is, and *you* are *that*!

◆   Nisargadatta said, 'A quiet mind is all you need.' And that's true. But he is not saying to try and *keep* the mind quiet, or attempt to sustain a period of quietness for some sort of attainment. For you can't 'get' there from there!

◆   Truly, there is nothing to be done—only to *see*.

◆   Relationships are not a gauge of who and what you are, however beautiful, moving and intriguing the other person may be: You are not a relationship. *You are a oneness that is without limit or form*. Savour the enormity of that fact. Though it is impossible to conceptualize, it is the actuality, right here and now. There is no working your way 'towards' it, or making yourself 'worthy' to obtain it. Indeed, you *can't* obtain it! You are *already* that. You are *already* that oneness without limit or form. There is nothing to do but to see it for yourself. Once this is understood, then everything else pretty much falls into place, including, of course, relationships.

◆ Stay with the fact that thoughts come and go; they are appearances and approximations, at best. They basically help us to communicate with others, and to live safely and productively while in this temporary human form. Thoughts, bodies and functions all change. But you are That which is aware of those appearances and changes. Zero in on just what that presence of awareness is. It is right here, right now. And that is the ultimate truth.

◆ If you really examine the issue, you will see that pauses are not just a component in non-duality, but are a part of practically any spiritual path. There has to come a moment when you are significantly and spontaneously paused. And in that timeless instant comes the possibility that you will perceive that you are nothing less than the pause itself. Then everything is clear! It's all there, whether there was some expansive or volatile moment preceding it or not. In that single second, your seeing is spot-on. *You are not witnessing or merging with anything*. Rather, you are timelessly perceiving that awareness has always been and will always be precisely who and what you *are*.

◆ There is this continuity beneath all things that are rising and falling in our lives—the thoughts, the feelings, the words, the events, the relationships—all of it. That continuity is there, **not** because it is doing anything or is actively attempting to maintain itself. It's there because that is what we **are**! It is our natural state. In a pause, we are able to discern that this is indeed the case. This isn't a way 'into' ourselves; there is no inner exploration going on. This is simply a recognition (though a magnificent one) of our fundamental nature. Awareness has **always** been there for the seeing. It's merely a matter of realizing that that is already the case.

◆ My silence is there whether I'm speaking or not. It's there whether I'm cleaning the bathroom or walking to work. There's nothing I have to do, focus upon, or manipulate. And it is utter nothingness, manifesting through this neurological labyrinth as deep, inexhaustible peace.

◆ Reflection is immensely more important than concentration or yogic postures when it comes to self-knowledge, especially when your reflecting is upon some choice non-dual pointer or passage. Then there is a possibility of your being genuinely paused by the words or pointer, and ultimately recognizing your natural state of being.

◆ *You are Freedom itself. No one can take you there. You can't even go yourself!*

◆ A thought is a neurological response containing information, whether it be sensory, creative, or mnemonic (memory-related).

◆ There is no such thing as a 'pure mind'. I don't care who claims it to be so. A thought, memory, or feeling (the very things that go to make the mind) are, by their nature, wayward, approximate, and misleading.

◆ Four great teachings arose in humanity's history: Advaita or Non-duality (India), Zen (Japan), Tao (China), and Mahayana Buddhism, known as the Great Vehicle, which some scholars consider to be an authentic rendering of the Buddha's teachings (India). The focus on each of these tenets is that self-realization can be had in anyone's lifetime.

◆ You are confused about your existence. No one believes that he or she does not exist. The issue is: What precisely are you existing *as*? You assume that you are your body or your brain or even your personality. But none of these things have any constancy. And your essence has to be constancy itself! And even that is inadequate, because you *are* Existence. Do you see what I'm saying? You *are* the thing that is being pointed to. You don't have a relationship with it at all. So we are speaking about that which is prior even to the concepts of relationship and constancy!

◆ The problem with spiritual paths is that they start with something—a chant, mantra, ritual, twirl, journey, meditation, mindfulness—you name it. But non-duality begins with nothing—or should I say, Nothingness. Non-duality contends that, from the very beginning, you are this unending Nothingness *already*. But this Nothingness is not a void; rather, it is a formless actuality that can be discerned and recognized through our bodies and minds.

◆ Nisargadatta's guru did not tell him to watch his thoughts, control his breath, raise his *kundalini*, or practise austerity. Rather, he simply but emphatically said: 'You are not what you take yourself to be. Find out what you *are*... Find your true self.' And Nisargadatta did just that.

◆ It is only when you realize that objects, people, and feelings, have a temporary existence, that you can have a detachment from them. This can't be done conceptually or by faith or brute determination. True detachment only comes with *understanding*. You cannot wilfully free yourself from these things. There can only be an easy and unwavering freedom from them through *understanding*.

◆ There is no true detachment from things or ideas or the world except through self-knowledge.

◆ True happiness is not joy, but detachment.

◆ There is no best way to come to this understanding. Some benefit from phone consultations, while others gain more from their own readingsand reflections. And then there are those who must have the personal, one-on-one conversation.

◆ You say that your meditation is all about 'embracing the present'. But how can you 'embrace the present' when you *are* the present? Further, the present doesn't move. So any action you want to take (meditative or mindful) is going to be a movement *within* this ever-present Present and, therefore, cannot be something connected with it, or fundamental to it.

◆ *Who* is thinking? Have you ever allowed yourself to truly sit with that question, to see it to its end? If you did, you couldn't help but come to the conclusion that there is no 'who' involved in the thinking. All there is are thoughts, suppositions and ideas, one following the other. It is a natural and much needed process in our lives. But the fact remains that *all that is going on is the thinking*: *There is no thinker!* This is the beauty of non-duality and of what you *are*, which is pure awareness. The thinking is arising *within* That.

◆   Awareness is not something that is 'above' us, or at some fairytale location. Nor is it chronologically arrived at. Somehow those ludicrous ideas are ingrained within our spiritual psyche—all the while we are the thing itself: immaculate Presence.

◆   Self-realization is amazingly simple. We complicate it, because we think it is an intellectual, methodological, or even ritualistic endeavour. And it is none of those things. It is merely *seeing* who and what you fundamentally are *at this very moment* and *not at some future date*. Besides, the 'future' is just a thought and a projection which, because of the attention you give it, causes you to bypass the obvious.

◆ Awareness *is*. So why isn't your focus there? You think that you have to 'do' something to your thoughts and thinking in order to become self-realized. But all of that is wasted time and energy. Go ahead and do those things, if you like. You have to discover the waywardness of your actions for yourself. You really have to come to the certainty that, 'Wait a minute—I'm being an idiot here!'

◆ Sorry, presence has no way or method to itself. The immediacy of it automatically negates both techniques or progressivism. You *are* awareness, so there is nothing to attain, and no technique in which to engage. See the elemental beauty of that. We are speaking about something that is directly before and within you *at this moment*. This *very* moment! *It is your natural state!* So, technically, you can neither hope to get to it, or hope to get out of it!

THE TEACHER

◆ A true teacher points to what is *already* present.

◆ You have to be careful about giving an inordinate focus on the teacher. For he or she is simply a mirror that is radiantly reflecting your own innermost nature.

◆ The task of the teacher is to remove misunderstanding. And this is done not by transmissions or by the giving of spiritual names, but by pointing to the immediacy of our natural and ever-present state.

◆ You need no special guru or lineage of teachers to help you awaken to your natural state. All that's required is a self-realized person (teacher or not) who directs you to Self with clarity, nuance, and self-assurance. It is Presence pointing to Presence.

◆ The only Guru is your fundamental nature, **your own presence of awareness**. Any genuine teacher you meet will simply be a personification of that presence. So you don't have to wait for a teacher or go to some great distance to meet one, in order to become self-realized. It's fine to do that if you want to. But keep this key point in mind: **You already are what you are seeking**. So there is absolutely nothing to attain.

◆ Alas, 99.99% percent of the teachers out there are not self-realized themselves. So all that they can offer you are... **practices**! But genuine non-dual authorities point from their own source to precisely what you are, which is the very same source. There is nothing overly spiritual or wishy-washy about these speakers and writers. They simply direct you, in any number of ways, to what is always **already** perfectly present.

◆ Non-realized teachers are simply people who are where they are. Some are honest about their lack of self-knowing; others are not. Some are well-meaning; others are manipulative.

◆ Fraudulent teachers go on and on about bliss and happiness. Real teachers point to **peace**.

◆ When it comes to this understanding, the teacher's ability to do anything is practically nil. *Self-knowing is done by yourself and with yourself*. No teacher does anything. Nothing! The true genius is the *teaching* and not in any particular person.

◆ *Your real teacher is your natural state*.

ॐ *THE SYLLABLE AUM (OM)*

◆   The syllable **AUM** has its own prominence: It is the first word in the first *Upanishad*. It is the substratum of all sounds; and it is perhaps the closest phonetic approximation of Presence that we have. And that some sage or sages recognized these facts even centuries before the *Upanishads* were written, is mind-boggling to me.

◆   The *Upanishads* were right (and brilliant!) to point out that **AUM** is a vibration that underlines all existence. For if we were to give presence a phonetic component, **AUM** would most definitely be it. But those *Upanishadic* authors and commentators who say that it must be chanted or mentally repeated (as a mantra) to attain self-knowledge, were wrong. Just ponder **A-U-M** carefully and silently, and allow it to show you what is **already** there, which is bare spaciousness and peace. **AUM** is one of those rare and wonderful words that both points to presence as well as approximates it.

◆   **AUM** is wrongly chanted to achieve enlightenment. But when that is being done, you are focusing on it as if it is something outside of or beyond you. Also, even a single chant is too much and entirely unnecessary. Just sit quietly and see that **AUM**—which the *Bhagavad Gita* beautifully notes, 'designates the Divine' and is 'heard throughout the universe'—is emanating from **within** you. Hear your own divinity. It is both present and silent, uttered and unsaid. And there is no place where it is not. It is the loveliest sound that you could imagine, and it is pouring—at this very moment—from your very own vastness.

◆   Certain recordings of **AUM** are amazingly moving and even pause-inducing. Rather than simply chanting along with such performances, see or notice that **AUM** is being uttered without cessation within you **at that very moment**. Allow the chanting to point you to that flawless and glorious fact.

◆   See the extraneousness of chanting, rituals, and practices. **AUM is there already before AUM is uttered**. All the great sages point to this fact—that you are **overlooking** your fundamental nature. You just need to be more attentive to this point. You really don't have to do anything other than that. For the 'doing' is in the **understanding**. But if you find joy in rituals and practices, then by all means enjoy them!

www.ingramcontent.com/pod-product-compliance
Lightning Source LLC
Chambersburg PA
CBHW030932090426
42737CB00007B/404